Lucky

Rachel Lewis

Dedicated to: Amanda B, Brett R, Jerrod B, Anthony S, Lou G, Dustin W, Bert L, Michelle L, Branden K, Brittany S

Contents

Chapter 1

Why Me?

I could never go back to a life of using.

Looking back, there are a lot of "Why me?" moments. At the time, it was "Why did I have to get caught?" "Why did I have to get ripped off" "Why don't my veins work" "Why me".

I know now that all of those moments and every day of darkness have led me to where I am now. Those hard times were all pieces to my broken road, paving my way to soberly-ever-after.

I often think now, "Why me".

Why me? Instead of the girl that shot up a little too much one night and never woke up.

Why me? Instead of the woman that tried to stop drinking, in hopes of a better life, and died in withdrawal?

Why me? Instead of the guy from my rehab that made it to sober life after opiate addiction, only to die from terminal cancer shortly after?

Why me? Instead of the teenager that tries pills for the first time and ODs?

Why me? Instead of so many....

There are a million reasons I shouldn't be here. There are a million times I could've easily been one on the list. My obituary printed in the finality of ink.

Why me?

Something, someone, somewhere, kept me safe. It could be as big as God, or as simple as karma. I was meant for more. I don't know who saved me or why, but I know I will spend the rest of my life making sure that it wasn't a mistake.

Chapter 2

Lucky?

Let me start by saying that I have never felt like a lucky one. Life started off feeling unfair. I was born in Cleveland Ohio, with my two parents. Nothing special. Dad worked for Ford for a long time before having back issues. And my mom worked for an eye doctor for as long as I can remember.

My first memories are of being with my Daddy. He loved to make spaghetti, and a mess along with it. He was my caretaker for my first years, as my mom worked full-time to provide. He had a bad back, but that never stopped him from letting me jump all over him. Remember when you could make the old TVs (way back in the 90s) play a channel on the big screen and then you could put another channel small in the corner? Yep, I had my Sesame Street in the small right-hand corner of the TV while he watched his shows. His laugh was contagious and so loud. He loved to fish and show me off to his friends. He was my daddy, and I adored him.

My parents didn't stay married very long. Although I was too young to even know what was going on. When I was 5 years old, I remember well that we were heading on vacation. My mom, her family, and I. And she picked me up from my dad's house a few days before our trip.

I was mad at my dad- why? I wish I could tell you. Something small, I'm sure. Maybe I couldn't get my turn of the big square on the tv? I yelled something stupid when I left his house like "I never want to see you again". A 5-year-old. Sassy & naive. The kicker is, I never saw him a gain.

The night before vacation with my mom, she told me my dad was on the phone.

"Hi Daddy"

"Hey Rachel, how's my girl"

"Good"

"I wanted to tell you I love you and to have fun on vacation with your mom and grandma and grandpa"

"I love you too"

The next day we piled in my grandpa's van to head for Colorado. It must've been a day after driving, we were somewhere in between where we started and where we were going, and my mom got a phone call. I feel like we stopped the van on the side of the highway... my mom got out as fast as she could. I can see her through the windows, pacing back and forth, kicking the ground with each step. My grandma gets out to comfort my mom and basically starts doing the same thing. As a 5-year-old, I didn't know what to think. What was happening? Why was she so sad and mad? The rest I must have blocked out of memory. But I know that my mom had the heartbreaking duty of telling me that my daddy, my best friend, had a heart attack and passed away. I didn't understand at first and tried to get back to him. I think she told me he was really really sick because I'm sure there's no right way to accomplish this task. And at a time before you could quickly Google instructions and advice. I can't even imagine how hard that must have be en for *her*. I tried begging for an airplane ticket to get back home, but he was gone.

My grandpa hadn't heard from him in a couple of days, went to his house to check on him, and he had passed in his sleep. Massive heart attack. Just like that..... life took my world.

We stayed one night in a random hotel, although I don't remember it, and headed back home to lay my Dad to rest. Little did I know then, this set the precedent for my entire life.

Chapter 3

The Stepped Up Dad

At the time of my dad's death, my mom was remarried to a man named Mark. Mark came with 3 kids around my age and they quickly made an addition together. We were sort of like the Brady Bunch. I was able to keep a strong relationship with my older sisters, from my dad's first marriage. So literally we were "his, hers, and ours".

To this day, my stepdad has been an enormous blessing in my life. He has answered every phone call and every text at every stage. I am beyond grateful for all the days he spent throwing the softball back and forth in the yard with me. For taking me to Girl Scout father/daughter dances. For never treating me as anything less than his daughter, yet never trying to usurp the place in my heart for my daddy.

I spent a lot of time playing outside. Riding bikes, rollerblading, and building forts. We had a lot of fun pets; cats, dogs, guinea pigs, snakes, turtles, hamsters, hedgehogs.

Life was as normal as it could be. We moved a lot in my early years, I lived in 7 houses before 2nd grade and went to 11 schools before graduation. I struggled with depression and anxiety. I struggled with my weight as a result of depression medicine. I struggled with feeling whole. I struggled with making friends and connections. I was always looking for more. I was always in trouble.

Chapter 4

Trouble

The first trouble with authority I can recall was in 7th or 8th grade. I was in my English class and the teacher stepped out. My friend at the time, grabbed the teacher's keys off her desk and threw them to me. I hid them in my purse. Later, I threw them down the hill behind our library. I didn't know what to do with them. I don't even know why I didn't return them but I was suspended for 3 days.

The next time I got in trouble with someone (other than my mom) was in 9th grade.

I had switched schools after 8th grade. My mom thought a new school would set me straight but it only made me more angry with life and I sought out all the rebels at my new school.

One day, I had my mom drop me and a friend off at the mall before she took my little brother to an event.

We were shopping in the cosmetics aisle when she started putting eyeliners and mascaras and lip gloss into both her purse and mine.

I don't think I had ever stolen from a store before. And I don't know that I even took anything other than what she put inside of my purse.

We went to walk out of the store and were told to stop. I did. She didn't. They called my mom who had to turn around and ruin my brother's day to come and get me from the security department of

Walmart. Being scolded in our minivan as we were pulling out of the parking lot, we saw my friend walking through high grass on the side of the road. We picked her up and drove her home and then I was grounded.

Chapter 5

Boys. Am I Right?

My first boyfriend was Rick, the bad boy in town. We lived in a small town where everybody knows everybody, and my mom went to school with everyone's parents.

I was 12 and Rick was 13. He was so funny and made me laugh constantly. He was goofy and didn't care what anyone thought. I was so drawn to that. My mom- not so much. We would meet at the library and sneak behind it to smoke cigarettes. I had him come over one night when no one was home and I heard my mom, stepdad, and brother get home as we were sitting in my bedroom. I said, "Hurry, get in my closet".

What was my plan? I had no idea. So my mom comes into my room, immediately knows I'm up to something, and found this boy in my closet. It looked so much worse than it actually was (haha).

She flipped out like you would not believe. Or if you're a parent, you might totally believe it. She dragged this kid back to his house and I was grounded. Again.

This caused so much tension between my mom and me. For years. I wasn't allowed to see Rick anymore. I saw him at school, and I'd call him when I went to my friend's houses. He was allowed to see any other girl, so it was hard for me and only made me want to be with him more. The more I tried to contact him, the more I got in trouble, and the more my mom saw him as a bad influence.

It was just too difficult.

Then I met my first love. His name was Beau. I was 14 at this time. The first thing I liked about him was that I was allowed to see him. He was so cute, a little quiet around others, and also a year ahead of me. He started coming over to my house and going to my softball games and we would go to youth group at church together. My friends loved him, my parents loved him, and I loved him.

He came to a softball game of mine and I was so smitten by his arrival that I completely missed my teammate throwing a ball at me and received my first black eye. The next day, we all went to an amusement park and I still have that season pass with the picture on it of me rocking a shiner.

Another thing that was great about Beau, was that his parents didn't care about anything we did. So on the days that I got to go to his house, we didn't have to stay in the living room in public spaces, like my mother's rule. His mom *offered* me cigarettes instead of throwing my difficult-to-acquire packs in the trash. His dad had severe health problems and was prescribed painkillers, which they also offered for fun. And it was.

Chapter 6

Finding More

I have always been searching for more. More feeling. More love. More needed. More happy. Just...More! I wasn't ever enough.

Beau and I stayed together for years. I grew fond of marijuana, which is pretty common in the boonies. A lot of my friends liked to drink, but I couldn't stand it. I would be at a party, everyone would have a beer in hand, and I'd sneakily pour it onto the ground a little at a time instead of drinking it. It was just so gross. It never held any appeal to me.

As we got older, Beau's dad's prescriptions got stronger. We graduated from chewing big Percocet 5s to sniffing the 15s. That felt good. There was my appeal. And it felt so innocent.

So many nights I would get dropped off at their house and his mom would assure my mom we would be monitored. As soon as the door closed though the trays of powdered pills would begin a steady rotation around the room. They used a Ped egg (for your feet) to grind the pills down faster. It was most always Percocet and OxyContin.

Sitting in his living room with his parents, watching movies, and snorting pills. And oh the passion and the love it ignited.

As well as this weird bond.

Beau and I moved in together after high school. His parents would come to visit and bring us pills sometimes. We drank with friends occasionally. We both held jobs and kept it together for a while. He had landscaping jobs and I worked for a telemarking company.

We broke up and I started nursing school, we got back together and I quit school.

Then the occasional pills just weren't enough.

We started buying the Perc 30s when we ran out of our monthly allotted amount that was supplied by Ma & Pa. Eventually we decided to live in a cheap trailer because we realized we would rather spend our money on drugs.

I managed a pizza place. I stole and inevitably lost my job. I also lost my car, which I once drove fresh off the showroom floor. $400 a month for a car payment was much better utilized in powder form. I drove a beater now, but it was free. His parents started to hate me- I don't even know if there is truth to that, or if he didn't want to share with me anymore. I wasn't allowed to join him at their house so I'd be left for hours and sometimes days wondering if they'd bought him off to leave me. Which he eventually did. I loved him something fierce. That first love which never seems to die.

Chapter 7

The Betrayer

When I was growing up, I had a unique pen pal.

My uncle Dave was incarcerated for basically my whole life. I was told that he had made some bad decisions that put him there.

We would take family road trips to visit him at his facility out of state. When we went there, he was loving and kind, he always had a Reese's cup waiting for me. Which was probably not easy to find in a place like that.

I remember vending machine burgers that didn't taste that great, scrabble and uno games and long sad hugs goodbye. In between visits, I'd be flooded with even more Reese's and thoughtful letters and cards with beautifully stunning artwork.

He was released after close to 20 years.

At the time that Beau and I were living in the trailer, I rekindled my relationship with my uncle. He was living just a few minutes away from us and I was often left at home alone while Beau was visiting his parents. My uncle and I grew close. He truly became my best friend.

One day, my worst fear came true, and Beau didn't come home. There was never much word as to the reasoning behind his absence and I was told to stop contacting him. His mom came to get his things from our trailer and I was crushed.

I don't think I could've gotten through that without my uncle.

He dragged me to his house and gave me his bedroom while he slept on the couch, where I stayed for what felt like weeks.

I was so depressed and it felt like he was the only one who cared.

As we spent more time together, talking and trading war stories; he learned of the pills that I had been using and I learned of the things that landed him in prison.

We were able to convey anything to each other without judgment. The transparency felt so refreshing.

There was one small problem... until now I had a constant supply of opiates. Everyone that we bought them from (when we didn't have the free ones from Beau's parents) was bought from *his* friends.

What was I supposed to do?

I know I'm going to get sick soon. I can't go too long without one, I'll go crazy!

I thought to myself: "Ok, I'll message his friend and see what happens." His friend readily invites me over. So I go there and establish my own connection.

At first, I was just trying to hold myself over because I was so used to having a steady supply. But they were expensive and I only had one connection which ran dry.

One day, I called the guy for some pills and he said that there were none around. He says he's picking up some heroin, it's cheaper and basically the same thing. My uncle hears this and is ecstatic. I am hesitant because the "H-Word" seemed so much worse than some medicine prescribed by a doctor!!

My uncle says: "I'll buy it, tell him we have $100".

This is where my life takes a drastic turn.

I'd love to tell you I said no. And, instead, I was sick for a few days and got over it. Kicked it cold turkey and moved on to bigger and better things, went back to school, got a degree, got a good-paying job where I was valued and doing the greater good, found a new better man, and lived soberly ever after.

But that is not my story.

Chapter 8

The H Word

At the time, "heroin" sounded so much more intense, and worse, than my pill problem.

But it was either start throwing up or give it a try. Plus, my uncle was with me and *he* knew what he was doing...right?

We got our batch and went back to his house.

I just wanted to snort it (that's what I was used to) and my pill guy said it was basically the same thing.

So I did.

My uncle took the same amount and said he wanted to shoot it. I was across from him at the kitchen table and watched him assemble this concoction. He tied his arm off with a rubber band and put the needle in his arm. He waited for a flash of blood, pushed down the plunger, and then he sat back and relaxed like I have never seen.

What did he just do?

He let out a euphoric sigh, "Ahhhh". Like he had just taken a sip of crisp Pepsi.

I sat there with my sniffles while he looked like he had just seen Jesus.

I was intrigued.

I asked a couple of questions about how different it feels and he offered to do it for me. I obviously had no idea where to begin. So there we were. And he did the whole thing for me. And I too, "relaxed" in a way that I never had before.

This was way better.

It's a hard thing to explain, they say the first time is always the best and you continue to chase it, never accomplishing that same high again. You sort of enter into an abyss, life slows down, your body slows down, the pain disappears, and it just felt good... it felt like nothing.

And without it, I felt pain. Sickness. Heartache. Lonely. Sad. Bored. S tuck.

I was always looking for more. And more, this definitely was.

It was thrilling in the beginning.

It was new, cheaper, and I got to do it with my pal. The cheaper part only lasts as long as your tolerance though. And well, I was depressed and trying to mask any possible feelings.

My uncle and I started selling our things for money, pulling scams, and using all of his monthly checks, and food stamps. Basically, there was no measure long or short enough that we were willing to go to get more H. The chase gave me something to live for at a time when I felt like I had nothing. At least I had a reason to get out of bed.

I ended up giving up my trailer since it was full of memories of Beau & me.

I got a job as a telemarketer again about an hour away and was making around $300 a week (if that). The days were long and I ran out of money fast. Having people yell at me to stop calling them for 8 hours was taxing and I was usually itching for a fix by the end of every shift.

As I was driving to work one day, I saw this sign: "Dancers & Servers Wanted, Come Inside". I don't know what possessed me to do it but

I pulled right in. It was a cabaret, and I'd be lying if I told you I knew what that meant prior to walking in. I opened the door and saw a man in a window that had the nasty stench of cigarette smoke pouring through it.

"Hi! I saw your sign!"

"You wanna be a server or a dancer?"

(Me- dance? Hahahahah)

"Server, Please!"

"How old are you?"

"20!" I stated proudly.

"You have to be 21 to serve alcohol..."

"Oh,..Ok...What about a dancer?" (I thought that I remembered how to do the electric slide)

"Ok, come on in." He then set off the buzzer that opened up the cabaret's official door.

Now listen, I have never been more shocked and uncomfortable in my entire life than in the following moments. When I walked through the door there was a bar and a lot of mirrors and one girl, wearing just a thong, slowly moving on a stage. I can't even call it dancing because it wasn't anywhere near the electric slide. Some management-type calls me into his office and I really can't look away because I'm like "What did I just get myself into?" I think for a hard moment..... "Ok, let's see what he says."

Upon talking with the manager, I learned that they have full-time shifts that they are looking to fill.

"Do you have experience?"

"Um, no."

"Take off your shirt." He orders with nonchalance.

"No!"

"Honey, they are gonna see your boobs."

Good point. Ok. Awkward. I guess I passed that test. (Wouldn't it be fun to know the requirements?) I tell him I have to hurry because my telemarketing shift is starting soon, he asks how much I make and I tell him and he enjoys a healthy chuckle.

Laughing, he says "You'll make $600 a day easy here." What!! You're lying. I didn't believe that at all- there was no way. So he gave me a chance to come in and "try" for 2 days- my days off from telemarketing. And he was right. I never went back to making cold calls.

Chapter 9

Dancing

S tripping. Exotic dancing. Pole dancing. Whatever name you'd like to give it...is a sport!

It took me a while to get "comfortable" doing this sort of thing. I *was* raised Christian after all, we went to church every Sunday with my grandma. And this was not what I thought I'd ever be doing.

The guilt of it all was easily masked by opiates. My good friend, Mr. H, who's company I could now afford to keep. There were older ladies there that had been dancing for over 20 years, were married, and were mothers. So it couldn't be *that* bad.

If you ever wondered just what it entails, let me enlighten you. There's not much "dancing" to be had. Maybe this differs by establishment, area, or popularity. But in this run-of-the-mill strip club, you stand on a stage for 2 songs. One of which you are in your outfit (which resembles a skimpy bikini) when the second song began we took our tops off. Pretty simple.

Yet it felt humiliating and degrading. The longest six minutes of my life. And then you waited your turn until you were back up again.

My first time on stage, I had "high heels" on. Maybe 1.5 inches? They laughed. There was a store across the street that sold essentials for this business so I just had to get some cash and run out for better shoes.

Apparently, I did not own the "high heels" the manager was referring to. Oh. The shoes are $80. So in my "low heels" and bikini (literally a tie-dye bikini, because where do you buy outfits ahead of time like this with $0?) I stood there with one hand on the pole and just swaying a little from side to side, maybe bent over?

Humilitingggggg.

Then all of the other dancers brought over dollars for me. That felt good. I was an outsider and so clueless about the ins and outs of this industry, this made me feel like I was accepted and doing something right. (I later learned that this is standard for everyone's first dance, haha, I wasn't special).

I earned the money for my shoes in no time and ran across the street to purchase them.

Ohhh 6 inches. So, that's what he meant. It was basically like walking on mini stilts.

I was given the stage name Bella, eventually mastered the art, and was able to afford my habit. I spent every dollar I made that night when I got out of work because I knew I'd make plenty more the next day. Private dances were much easier to learn. $20 for the length of a song, and you sit on their lap and move around. Easy peasy. And I get off my feet!

A lot of the "customers" pushed the boundaries after a while. Some girls were ok with more contact for more money. And others knew the guys outside of work. There were so many outlets to cash under one roof.

I started living with my mom again, her house was much closer to the club than my uncle's. She knew what I was doing but distanced herself from it. I stayed in the basement mostly and worked opposite hours. I met a few people at the cabaret that were willing to meet me outside of work and give me much more money for much less time. At this point, the 8-hour shifts were just too much. I was tired. I was tired of being someone I wasn't. I was tired of listening to these guys say things I didn't want to hear. I was tired of wearing 6-inch heels and not much of anything else. So I quit.

For quite a while, I was able to meet my regular guys to do favors for, make my cash in an hour instead of 8, and go on my merry way.

I cannot tell you the many times I cried while doing these favors. I tried so hard to pretend it was just a boyfriend and that it wasn't a big deal. But I lost a little part of me in each hotel room.

A lot of times, I would be on the verge of withdrawal at the time. Withdrawal from an opiate is like a cyclical flu that you know is coming every 8 hours, and you have to find the medicine to cure it. You get physically ill: sweating, vomiting, diarrhea, fever, and your mind screams: "YOU HAVE TO FIX THIS NOW AND YOU KNOW HOW!"

Sounds sexy, right?

Chapter 10

My Dance With The Devil

I sold my soul and everything else I had for something that never once loved me back.

By this time in my life, I wasn't getting "high". I wasn't having fun. I had no material values and anything I did own that held any sort of equity quickly went to pawn shops or was converted into gift cards that I could sell for ½ of their worth. I was skinny because I rarely ate. I had pushed away everyone I loved because I had probably stolen from them or passed out on their couch during some holiday party.

Some days I had no money, and no guys to meet before my sickness came on. It was 8 hours for a long time. I learned to count the hours after I did a shot so I knew how long I was ok before I was sick again. I tried to always pull the next scam or anything I could come up with to keep the pain at bay.

I remember the day I sat home alone at my mom's house and googled "How to shoot heroin". I learned the basics, without my uncle's assistance, and got my needle, and said: "Let's go."

I struggled with this from the start. It was hard. It hurt. I have small veins that seemed to give up after one go. I was covered in bruises and needle marks and old dried blood on any given day. If you don't get the needle in your vein just right, it turns into a hard bubble that hurts for days and doesn't enter your system the same. A waste. But I tried and tried and tried. I found a few good veins that I could use and did my best to rotate around them.

I don't remember much from this sliver of time going forward.

Over the next year, I pretty much lived in my car. I think my mom finally caught me with H. I had so much of my own stuff going on, I rarely talked to my uncle anymore. That meant I would have to share.

I had no friends, not a single one. Only people I bought my supply from. And they were friendly enough.

I slept in McDonald's parking lots and Flying J's. I needed somewhere I could go to the restroom in the morning.

I remember this time when my mom came to visit me. I was about an hour from her house, where most of my connections were. We went to the Goodwill. We had a good time together, but I remember when I went to try on a shirt and for one small moment forgot how big of a mess of a human I had become, and went down to short sleeves in front of my mom. She saw my arms that were bruised and beaten and I quickly covered them back up and we didn't talk about it. But I knew she saw it.

She was heartbroken that I was living in my car.

I'm not sure, I think this was the same day (it could've been at a different time) but she had rented me a hotel room for a week. Don't even for one second think that it was the Hilton. Quite the contrary. Nevertheless, I was completely thrilled about having a bed and a place to go to the bathroom every morning. It was so cheap, maybe $100 for the week. In the midst of this tumult, I would never spend that chunk of change on anything other than my fix.

I had also acquired this little dog as well. No, big dog. Sometimes I got lucky and was able to stay the night at places where I bought my stuff from. One time was with this girl from school and her boyfriend. I stayed with them for a few days. One of the days, her neighbor let me know that they were putting these Doberman puppies outside for free and I said: "No! Give me one!" (I couldn't even take care of myself!)

So here I am at this point in life carting my playful puppy around, homeless, broke, and packing a heroin addiction.

I remember having the dog at the motel as well. It was so nice to have a home base for a while. I think I paid for a week after that too because I couldn't imagine going back to my car.

Chapter 11

The Good Friend

I met Brad at the cabaret and he was my favorite customer.

He was nice and easy to talk to, also funny, and adored me. It was just easy to be myself with him, instead of having to put on the act I portrayed with all of the others.

Shortly after getting together outside of the club, he began to learn of my addiction. Mostly because we met in nice hotel rooms where it looked much more appealing to do my shots instead of some Burger King parking lot.

He helped me out every chance he got. He bought me food, clothes, and dog food for the puppy. He even helped me buy my brother a basketball for his birthday party and provided transportation.

It was just easy with him because he was like a boyfriend. He had a history of addiction before we met, and soon indulged with me. He never shot up but preferred snorting. This became beneficial for me because he had money and now he wanted back into the game. He kept me afloat for a while. Later you will see why he is "the good friend".

Chapter 12

Rock Bottom

I bounced around from hotel rooms to parking lots to random couches to the back of my car.

A few months later, I grew too tired.

I had danced at 3 establishments by this time. My veins had all been shot out. I couldn't even do dope when I got it. I would cry because I was so ill. I had the antidote in the palm of my hand, but couldn't get it in me. After succumbing to defeat I would end up snorting it, which had half of the effect on me. Allaying sickness became expensive. The car was frigid at night and my body was tired of being my only source of income.

Welcome to rock bottom.

I reached out to my mom and told her I needed help. She sat with me so many times and held me in withdrawal. We researched rehabs and detox and home methods and tried to figure this out, but it was taking too much time. I was so sick. She witnessed it firsthand. And when I was sick, I didn't care about anything else but putting a stop to it. Stuck on the toilet with a trash can in my lap to throw up in. Chills. Sweats. It is by far the worst disease I've ever gone through. And it was persistent.

I didn't want to talk to anyone while I was fighting the pain and I used this time to create my survival plan to get sober. It was such an exhausting period in my life and was so hard on my mom. My hero, and despite everyone telling her what was right and wrong, she never left my side and always helped me in the best way that she knew. And I wouldn't change a thing. We realized that we couldn't afford rehab alone. I needed to detox. Fast. Before I got too sick.

Chapter 13

Brighton

Although we did not have the money to afford rehab, we thought that if I told my Grandparents what I was going through, maybe they would help.

Yes, read that again. Grandparents. Going and telling them what I was going through.

Not a fun day.

I remember sitting outside of their house and telling them that I was not the person that they saw smiling during Christmas. That I had been truly struggling to survive, and had a terrible problem with opiates. They wanted to know how I had been affording it all this time. And, although I tried to tiptoe around it, everything pretty much came out.

"I do favors for favors."

Something you never want to admit to your grandparents.

I begged for help and they agreed to do so. They had two conditions: One, I would complete a full 30-day inpatient rehab program. Two, the rehab had to be out of state. This was smart because they knew that I had several connections in the area, and were concerned that in a moment of weakness, I would reach out to get a ride to leave rehab.

The only problem was that I needed to go to detox somewhere *today* or I was going to use. I had to.

They allowed me to go detox at nearby Laurelwood Hospital while they figured out where I'd be going for an inpatient program afterward.

Laurelwood was good to me and was my first experience with detox, rehab, and AA meetings.

Largely for the first few days, I felt like death. I don't remember much more outside of sitting in the hospital room getting sick and waiting for it to end.

Sometimes I'd venture out of the hospital room to smoke a cigarette with another 1 or 2 people who seemed to be going through the same thing. Most would stay at this hospital for the rehab program that followed detox, but not me. I was waiting to be swept away out of state.

I don't think I knew where I was going until the day of. Not that I was familiar with any of these establishments anyways.

I called my mom on the 5th morning and she told me that they had decided on a rehab center in Michigan. Only 3 hours from home, making it easy for her to drive and visit. This was the longest stretch of sobriety for me in years. It was scary and I needed my mom.

After I finally felt like a physical human being again, she picked me up from detox and we drove straight to Brighton Hospital, Michigan. Apparently, this is one of the finest rehab centers in the country, and although I had never heard of it—I had heard of Eminem, who also had been a patient there.

What?

Rehab was life-changing in so many ways.

But we'll get to all that.

The first few days were uncomfortable and I missed my life and I missed my mom and just wanted to go home. There were people of all ages, ranging from 18 to 80, all struggling with every addiction you could imagine.

We went to classes, meetings, and therapy. It was a full-time schedule of learning how to be sober. From sunrise to sunset. Different than anything I'd ever done.

It was my first time attending AA meetings.

I quickly found friends though. Actual people that cared about how I was feeling and doing every day. The common ground we found through addiction created a strong bond between us all.

These were the first "friends" I'd had in so long.

And we formed relationships, considering all the personal horror stories we shared in therapy or otherwise.

I got to rap with my roommate (Hey Katie!). Who is still my friend to this day. (yes, I said rapped- must be something in the air there hahaha).

It was interesting to meet people from all over that had taken the same tour through hell that I had. Some were new to the world of addiction. Others, back for their 10th stay; all of them, desperately seeking more.

Although you were not allowed to fraternize or have romantic relationships, it is inevitable. You're amongst a bunch of adults, men, and women, who have suppressed all of their natural desires for so long with one thing or another, that are finally feeling things again. It's only natural that romance, love, lust, and the yearning for companionship be part of those feelings. All of your teenage hormones come rushing back. So here we are again...boys. Am I right? (Forehead slap).

Chapter 14

My Person

S ometimes, you just meet that person you can't live without.

As I was getting used to the routine of my new sober life in rehab, I started spending a lot of time with a guy named Dan.

Dan was so different from anyone I'd ever known.

Right from the start—he was the one that everyone gravitated to. He was funny, smart, worldly, and 8 years older than I was, and just seemed to get me.

It's funny looking back because I was so oblivious.

I would tell him about my past, and he'd tell me about his. We would sit on a concrete wall in the backyard and bond by singing country songs. When I woke up in the morning to go outside for my first cigarette, there he would be, standing there holding one of his hoodies. I think it took me a really long time to realize that it was especially for me, in case I got cold.

At meal times, the men and women were separated, but he always made me a rehab cocktail (apple, orange, and pineapple juice maybe?)

In those moments though, I really wasn't focused on boys. I didn't think anyone would want to be with me after hearing of all the things I had done.

30 days in rehab probably don't seem like a long time to the average person, but it felt like the equivalent of 6 months normal time.

My mom would come to visit me on the weekends, and I remember showing her who Dan was and telling her about our close friendship and she met a few of my girlfriends as well.

I can't remember exactly when our relationship turned into more... I remember going to the AA meetings instead of NA meetings (alcoholics anonymous vs narcotics anonymous) because it was basically the same thing, but Dan was in AA.

The days I once counted down in excitement to leave this place became days that I wished were longer because soon our time together would be up.

He knew everything awful about me and still wanted to be there for me every day. The elevator became our kissing booth, and the guys would help sneak me into their TV lounge so we could be together. We were so raw, open, and honest with each other, and had this weird trauma bond. I felt safe with him. I felt like we were a good match, even though it is vehemently recommended against.

Do you know what they tell you to get out of rehab?

A plant.

Not a boyfriend.

Our stay was coming to an end. He was leaving about a week before me and was going to stay in a halfway house nearby (his parents also lived 3 hours away from Brighton in the opposite direction).

I decided I should do the same.

I'll be honest with you- I just couldn't imagine ever letting him go.

Chapter 15

The D

It started off pretty well.

My mom came up to get me set in my new halfway house. She brought my Doberman puppy to visit me and let me say goodbye before rehoming her.

I lived in a women's halfway house and Dan was at a men's house about 20 minutes away.

We talked a lot on the phone, and he would pick me up to go to meetings together.

The women's halfway house was nice. We had a roommate and shared a bathroom and kitchen. We had chores to do around the house. The woman that ran it lived upstairs. We were able to sign out to leave for meetings and things and had a curfew, drug tests, and someone keeping an eye on us. There was a constant flow of new people, as others checked out or got bounced quite frequently.

It was a struggle to regain a normal state of humanity.

I was both newly 21 and newly sober, living away from my family and everyone I knew that wasn't from rehab.

It wasn't long before I resumed my search for more.

I couldn't stand being with myself and my thoughts. I tried alcohol first and really tried to like it. I was legally allowed to buy it for the first time ever, so I was able to sample things that were smoother than natural light. I would desperately try to get drunk to mask any feelings. And alcohol would be out of my system soon for the drug tests. It wasn't my problem drug anyways. And although that is true, it just opened the trapdoor for me to sink even deeper.

One day, I called a girl that was in rehab with me and asked if she could get any H.

Nothing had ever been so easy.

She gave me a phone number and I called it. A man answered and told me to come to some random intersection in Detroit and call him when I was there.

Detroit is about 30 minutes from Brighton. I knew absolutely nothing about Detroit, or this guy I was meeting. But I had some money that I probably lied to get a hold of. So I drove to Detroit, called the guy, and his car pulled up behind mine. I got out of my car and into his, we "met", did our transaction, and parted ways.

It didn't take long for me to spiral out of control.

Maybe a month.

My veins had time to recover during rehab and had become more cooperative. I wasn't using it all the time, so I wasn't getting sick when I didn't have it.

And I hadn't ever had a connection like this before.

It was better quality, less money, and always available. My room-mate at the halfway house at the time was also back to using H, and we both soon got kicked out for having needles. I, of course, put the blame on her and I'm sure she did the same.

I could've found another sober home, or gone home with my mom, but my heart was stuck on Dan. He was now this huge part of my life and I couldn't imagine walking away from that. So this guy calls his parents and says he's coming home and (bonus!) bringing a girl from rehab to live with them.

I bet they were ecstatic.

Chapter 16

Jail

Have you ever been?

I 10 out of 10 do not recommend it.

My first experience being arrested was not my fault.

I know, I know.

But it really wasn't!

I was 17, in high school, and had a friend Mickey that lived 10 minutes away.

He mostly smoked weed with me and we kind of dated for a little while but we were mainly just friends.

He knew a ton of people that I didn't. And one night, he said. "Let's go hang out with Bobby & Jane".

"Ok."

I was the only one with a car so we drove over there and as soon as we pull into the apartment complex, Bobby & Jane (maybe 2 others?) are all riled up about so & so coming to start a fight.

I didn't know these people, or what was going on.

They told us to hurry and come up to their apartment. One of them held either a knife or bat in their hand.

Any normal person would probably have been long gone at this point, so I guess my fault lies there.

Instead, I go with Mickey upstairs to this apartment with these crazy people and they turn off the lights and are basically hiding. The girl, Jane, has blonde hair that is saturated red with blood. She and I go to the bathroom where I tried to clean her up.

I had no clue as to what had happened or even whose blood that was. I don't think it was hers.

Within a few minutes, police officers are banging on the door. Yelling. Everyone is quiet and hiding inside the apartment.

This lasted for a while until the police finally busted in the door.

We were all arrested and taken down to the police cars. No one even asked my name until I was processed. It was quite an adventure. I was so scared.

They told me that I could make a phone call....

"Mom? It's me. I'm in jail."

"WHAT FOR? What are you being charged with?????"

(Good question)

I ask the lady who is monitoring my call.

"Felonious assault and kidnapping." She informs me.

I repeat it to my mom, She about chokes.

"Mom I swear I didn't do anything!!"

She tells me she will get me an attorney and to hold tight.

So there I am. This child, in this hardcore city jail, with all these people covered in blood that I am associated with.

They put me into a cell with Jane.

At this point, I just wanted to go to sleep. There was a metallic bunk bed and toilet next to it. And a big gate in front of that. I remember telling Jane that I had to pee, and she said: "Don't forget to wave at the camera". Which I thought was just a joke because I assumed that we were being watched with everything we did. So I was like yeah haha and went to the bathroom, with a camera staring at me.

It wasn't until early the next morning that I saw a sign that said: "wave to the camera before using the restroom". Apparently, that wasn't a joke, and the guards will look away. Hahahahaha. Oops.

Once my attorney came, it was easily cleared up that I had nothing to do with the assault and barely knew the names of the people that did. I was released after maybe 18 hours. I don't know what happened to everyone else. I know that Mickey was also released for not being involved. Apparently the "kidnapping" comes from not opening the door to the apartment when the police ordered.

I wish I could say that scared me straight, and was my only excursion behind bars. But it was only the beginning.

Chapter 17

Jail #2

While we were living with Dan's parents, we made a lot of stupid mistakes.

We sold tools and jewelry for money, we used credit cards that didn't belong to us.

I think we got ourselves kicked out of there too.

One of the dumbest things we had done was to think we could steal jewelry from a popular retail store and pawn it off after.

We drove to just outside Detroit (where we sometimes slept in the car so we didn't have to drive 3 hours back home because we were close to the dealer).

Sometimes, we were able to pawn or steal enough for a crappy hotel room for a week.

But at this point we just needed money.

We formulated a plan, went to this superstore, parted ways and I don't even know what we ended up with.

I know I had a women's watch in my underwear.

We managed to grab a few things each and went to walk out of the store. Before we could breach the exit we were asked to stop by an "undercover shopper" that had been following us and watching the whole time.

We ran and hopped in the car as fast as we could.

I remember Dan driving backward out of the parking lot so they couldn't read his license plate. We may have actually pulled this off..... except we were completely out of gas. We drove as far as we could, stopped at a gas station, continued to try to go on our way, and were pulled over shortly after.

I remember it was a woman officer that talked to me.

They separated me and Dan.

What was I supposed to say? Do? Am I going to jail? What did we do? We didn't plan for this.

During this time, I had a women's watch band pinching my hoo-ha and this officer says she knows we stole this and that and asked where it was.

I tried telling her we ditched everything but she didn't believe me.

As I was being put in the back of the police car, I realized this was happening with or without this watch in my crotch; so I confess and ask her, "Ok- can I get this watch out of my pants?" I couldn't imagine sitting down on that plastic car seat with that thing in my underwear.

Ouch!

We were definitely going to jail. And I deserved it.

This time was absolutely horrible.

Not that any stay in jail is a 5-star experience.

We had pulled this scam because we were sick and needed a fix. And instead of copping successfully, we're now sick, absent a fix, and in jail.

Details henceforth are scattered at best.

I remember seeing Dan walk by calm as a cucumber while I was panicking.

But that's how I got when I was in withdrawal. Remember: I know the cure, and I need it now! I was growing sicker by the second and locked inside of an "observation cell", a glass box right by the guard's station.

By myself.

I called both of our parents and begged them to bail us out.

After much crying, arguing, pleading, and manipulating, my mom drove 3 hours in the middle of the night to bail us out.

She took us back to the hotel room, scolded us, and went home.

They had impounded his vehicle and we were paralyzed in dope-sick.

I don't know how we had any money left, but I remember calling a car service,(this was before Uber), and a nice black car came to pick us up at the hotel and take us to our destination in Detroit.

We only had money for one way. But who cared, just so long as we can make it to the dealer.

Now remember, when I am really sick, I'm stuck on the toilet with a trash can in my lap. So now I'm in this fancy black car where the guy had been courteous enough to provide snacks in the middle of the back seat and two little mini bottles of water.

He probably remembers me as much as I remember him.

I had to ask him to pull over 20 times on the drive as I could not stop throwing up. I had a bag at one point that was leaking my vomited yellow bile all over his floor mats.

It was horrific.

But we made it and got our fix plus a little more for later.

We felt human again but had no vehicle and were 15 minutes away from the hotel.

We attempted to take the City bus. This turned out to be a darkly hilarious endeavor. We got on, paid for both of our day passes under the impression it would get us to our destination, and the bus went about 5 miles (maybe) before they announced on the loudspeaker: "End of the line".

Every single person gets off.

What does the end of the line mean???

We dejectedly shuffled off and walked the rest of the way.

Chapter 18

The Break-Up

I 'm still not clear as to what had happened.

I have a lot of holes in my memory from this time in my life; as you can imagine.

But Dan and I parted ways.

I'm not sure if we really broke up or if we just had to find somewhere to live and couldn't find a way to do it together.

He stayed with a friend from school, near that area, and I somehow found my way to Brad's house back in Ohio.

Brad, the good friend, had become a painter.

He had his own company and was always busy doing big jobs on fancy houses.

He let me stay with him for a while and gave me his bed while he slept on the couch. I needed money and he needed help with jobs.

Was I a painter?

Absolutely not, but I also wasn't a stripper and pulled that off so I was pretty confident in my self-efficacy at this point.

I never expected to love it so much.

Painting was fun!

To start in an empty room and completely change it with your own two hands was such a thrill. An accomplishment. Like I was actually doing something worth doing! I was really good at it and was able to contribute a lot at jobs. I could handle an entire room while he worked in another. I didn't really care about getting paid in cash, I just wanted to go to the dealer afterward. And he'd take me.

I worked for a while for him like this and we had a lot of fun together.

Painting brought me so much joy.

But of course, that wasn't enough. At some point, I had stolen Brad's laptop and traded it for heroin to our dealer.

Yes. Our shared dealer.

Brad knew it was me but I denied it of course. (He later bought it back from the dealer, quite the businessman). He did file charges against me but we moved on.

I had a warrant for petty theft. But again, who cared?

Chapter 19

The Day I Died

My next memory of the good friend wasn't long after that.

I was sitting in his bedroom, getting my syringe and liquid concoction together, while he was in another room of the house.

This was during the advent of fentanyl's demonic arrival.

Dealers were lacing tiny quantities in their heroin or cocaine or anything really, to make you more addicted and make the high feel stronger.

Was it cheap? I wasn't so sure.

You could feel it though when it was in your stuff, the potency was palpable.

I did my normal amount, said "fentanyl" and my next memory is gasping for air with Brad on top of me.

I didn't know what was going on.

Brad said I wasn't responding and he had to call 911.

My first thought was "No!! I have a warrant" and I got up and tried to run.

I made it maybe 2 feet before I fell on my face.

Barely alive, I was soon being checked by EMS. I tried so hard to avoid giving my name, which didn't work. And I was arrested. Again. (Third time)

Sitting in a jail cell, I suddenly hurt so bad on my sides and my chest. I lifted up my shirt and saw that I was completely bruised on my ribs.

I was so confused.

What happened?

I'll tell you what happened. The good friend saved my life. Despite what I had done to him, despite putting his career and freedom in jeopardy, despite every possible consequence, he gave me chest compressions to keep my heart beating to save my life. There's not a day that goes by that I'm not grateful to him. Most people in this situation would've left me to die.

This probably should've scared me into sobriety again, but it didn't.

Vaguely, I remember getting put into this large room with about 30 women, with metal bunk beds all over the room. There were toilets and showers in the back corner and a tv was on, playing the movie "Columbiana". There were girls sitting at the tables watching the movie and I was given a top bunk, which I already knew would complicate the inevitable withdrawal coming my way, but I couldn't really complain. I also learned that as soon as you say you're going to be sick or you're in withdrawal, that you'll be put in a cell by yourself sans TV, and with no other humans, which would make the time slug by even slower; so I didn't say anything.

In the middle of the night I woke up intensely vomiting and was taken into my own cell. I wasn't there for long, maybe 3 days.

I think Brad might have even bailed me out.

I don't know where I went from there, I didn't think I was welcome back to Brad's house.

Can you blame him?

Chapter 20

Short Stories From A Damaged Memory

At some point, Dan and I moved into an apartment together.

We had stayed in touch this whole time and were tired of driving 3 hours to see each other since he had been in Michigan while I was in Ohio.

It was a really crappy, cheap, studio apartment.

He had a good job and I was painting with Brad sometimes. But we were together and that's all that mattered. We owned nothing of value because we'd rather get high.

One day, when we were doing our shots together in our apartment; Dan fell over. Straight back, stiff as a board. I was yelling at him and he was blank.

Then he started turning blue.

I was really high at this time, so I didn't even know he was overdosing when he was. (Which I bet is how 90% of overdoses happen).

My mom worked across the street from my apartment and I called her and said come over now. She got there in a few minutes and Dan's lips were completely blue. She told me, "CALL 911!"

I don't remember if I did or if she did.

They gave him a shot of Narcan and he popped up completely normal.

What in the world?

We were taken to the hospital where he could get checked out. I felt so screwed up and I couldn't stay awake in the hospital room and we just wanted to leave.

I don't think it ever hit either one of us that he had just died.

Right there.

Right in front of me.

But we didn't care about anything.

•Many times we didn't have any money and would go to a gas station and park by the gas pump. I would get out and put on my most normal face and walk up to strangers, give a good story, and ask for some cash.

"I left home without my wallet and just need $5."

"I have to pick up my kids from daycare and just ran out of cash." (I didn't have kids)

"Could you spare a couple of dollars, tomorrow is my payday." (I didn't have a job)

You'd be surprised at the generous nature of common folks. Some days it was enough to get by.

•In Detroit one day when Dan and I were sick and going to pick up our usual 12 packs for $100, I called the magic phone number as usual and the guy was really rushed and short with me. All I could make out is "S O 4".

I hung up the call and Dan asked, "So where am I parking?"

"Um... S O 4?" I answered with little conviction.

After about 15 minutes of arguing and fighting and feeling too stupid to call the guy back for clarity even though he said it 5 times.

We drove and we saw the intersection of Edsel Ford and just looked at each other in cadence like "Ohhhh".

SO4.

We found it.

•Suboxone

I was on suboxone following rehab.

Suboxone is an opiate suppressor that tricks your brain into thinking that it has had it's fix.

It will also make you ill if you use opiates while you're on it.

I had to see a specialist every 30 days, give a urine sample to make sure I wasn't using, and pay a lot of money to get the prescription.

My mom paid for most of them.

I quickly found out that they were worth money to people I knew and that I could trade them to the dealers for H. Also, that I could stop using H, allow for the beginning stages of withdrawal to proceed, pop a suboxone, and be ok.

Passing drug tests was also a cinch.

I bought fake urine from head shops, kept it in my underwear, and would slyly pour it into the sample cup without anyone ever suspecting anything.

I grew to become used to taking drug tests.

My mom had drug tested me all throughout growing up.

She could always read right through me though.

In school, one of my friends was also trying to pass her mom's home drug tests and took a bunch of niacin vitamins and offered me some.

I hadn't a clue as to what they were or what they would do, but standing in the girl's bathroom I took a handful.

About an hour later, I was called out of class and brought to the nurse's office where my friend who gave me the pills and another mutual friend were waiting for me to join the conversation.

We were all purple.

Our skin had literally turned purple. Our faces were steaming hot and we were itching with restlessness. It was an awful feeling.

"Do you want to tell me what niacin is?" the nurse interrogated.

I thought, "No...but do you want to tell me?!"

We all played stupid.

I suffered through this episode multiple times after that, trying to cleanse my system of marijuana before my mom tested me. I would try bio freeze to soothe the burn it made me feel all over my body, but that just clashed heat and ice.

I also discovered drinks that you could buy to clean out your system for a small window of time. They were awful and thick and sugary. You had to chug it within a couple of minutes and you had to time it just right for your upcoming test because it would only keep you clean for a few hours.

•I was painting with Brad on a job one day when he told me about a raccoon problem in the attic of his house. He had been trying to trap them for weeks and finally got a baby. He showed me pictures and I thought that it was the cutest little thing.

On our lunch break, we stopped by his house so I could see it and I gave it a banana in his front yard through the cage/trap and the little baby raccoon's hands just melted my heart and I. Took. This. Thing. Home.

To that tiny crappy apartment.

She slept on our heads and scratched us with her really long nails. She was super cuddly at first and loved avocados and bananas and berries. But she pooped all over and was getting stronger; she was soon able to open up the refrigerator by herself. She got into frozen blueberries and ate a pound of ground beef and then we realized that *maybe* she needed more than a tiny apartment. (Duh)

Chapter 21

Jail #3

For one reason or another, I was driving Dan's vehicle.

A truck.

I don't believe that I had a car at the time and I don't recall why.

One day, like any other, I went to meet one of my dealers about 20 minutes from the apartment.

The dealer would also just give you a name of a street to park on, and shortly after he would sidle up behind you.

We did our deal.

I didn't have much money this time, only enough for one shot and I was sick. By the time I had finally got my stuff, I couldn't wait the 20 minutes to drive back home. I needed to feel better NOW. I pulled into a drug store parking lot and started getting ready for relief. I opened the console which had various used needles and tools for use. I struggled with my bruised, broken veins and finally got it.

Ready for this?

The next thing I know, no less than 10 police officers wake me up banging on the windows of the truck. I open my eyes and freak out because that's a lot of cops. I look over and saw that I had a needle hanging out of my arm, and several others in an exposed console that they are staring at.

How long had they been there?

Did I fall asleep?

I found out that one of the drugstore customers called them on me, which also probably saved my life.

Of course, I was arrested.

And the truck was impounded.

I think this was my longest jail stay, to date. I was charged with "drug instruments" for the syringes. I thought I was lucky because I didn't have any actual heroin left to be charged with. So at least it was just that. I think I was there for 3 days. Enough to get super sick but not completely through withdrawal and detox. I bailed out and went back to my ways. Now with court date looming in the short distance.

The morning I went to court, I gave my name and sat in the courtroom with about 20 others waiting for the judge. My name was called by a man in a suit off to the side of the room. I stood up and he asked me to come with him and introduced himself as my public defender. He took me to a room between the courtroom and the front entrance and said, "You are here to answer to charges of drug instruments?"

"Yes." I beamed proudly.

"I wanted to let you know, there's an additional charge of possession of heroin being added to your case today"

"What?!? That's wrong, I didn't have any heroin" I argued.

He informed me that they tested the residue inside the needle, which came back as heroin, therefore I was charged with possession.

"So...what does that mean?" I asked incredulously

"You will be arrested for the new felony charge when you go in front of the judge in a few minutes" But then he adds, "Or...you can leave."

"I can leave?" I asked in amazement.

"Yes, but you'll have a warrant."

Sold.

I left.

No way was I going to jail that day.

Chapter 22

Warrants

I now had multiple warrants waiting for me and spent a few months dodging them.

Dan and I were living together, both unemployed.

At one point, police officers started showing up at my mom's house and other places I was known to stay, looking for me after failing to appear in court.

I refused to go back to jail. I wasn't going to be sick. I didn't have heroin the day I got arrested and refused to be charged with it.

Around this time I was prescribed suboxone.

Suboxone, in a nutshell, is a methadone alternative. If you take it every day as prescribed, you will not go into withdrawal. It fools your brain into thinking you had your opiate and you go on with your life. I was only on it for a few months, and I only took it correctly less than that. I was mostly selling my prescription to get more H. In theory, it does sound like a good idea, a safer alternative; but it wasn't a good fit for me. It just masked my problems and gave me an outlet for more cash.

Chapter 23

Pivot

One night, I was sitting with Dan while he talked to his brother on the phone. His brother had a good-paying job with Lawrence County in South Dakota and had extended an offer for us to come stay with him and his wife and he would get Dan set up with a job.

I somehow graduated high school without ever taking a geography class, but I was certain South Dakota is nowhere near Ohio.

At first, it sounded insane.

But then it sounded like a way out of this rat race I had been living in. I couldn't keep dodging my warrants. We didn't have any money and barely had a place to stay.

This *could* be a fresh start.

I was going to wait until I got my suboxone prescription and then we would buy a bus ticket to South Dakota. I had never met the people I was going to live with, and was leaving everything I knew behind.

We packed one bag each and headed for the Greyhound station.

Saying goodbye to my mom that day was heartbreaking. I had never been away from her that far with no return in sight.

But being behind bars seemed like the only alternative.

So I put all of my faith and trust into Dan and the promise of our new life together.

We got on the bus, I think it was a 35-hour drive. Long and uncomfortable, and I was nervous about what was to come. But hopeful.

When we got to our final destination, Dan's brother Brian picked us up and took us back to his house. I met his wife, Michelle. We were shown a room in the house where we could stay. Dan even started working first thing the next morning, which was great.

Except. It wasn't great for me.

Remember, I grew up in the country—farms, fields, 30 minutes to the nearest Walmart. Then lived in the big cities—Cleveland & Detroit. And had adapted to being around lots of people, places, and stores.

This was new.

This was frigid mountain ranges, desolate hills, and vast loneliness.

My cellphone stopped working on the drive-up because the Ohio service I was using didn't cover South Dakota and I had to get a new phone. I didn't have a car. I was in a weird town, with people I didn't know. And Dan was so happy with his new job and being with his brother.

It was awkward to be at home all day with this woman I had just met. I couldn't wait for Dan to get home from work. I was also struggling with not using. We kind of intentionally screwed ourselves when we got on the bus because we knew we wouldn't be able to get any more heroin, at least not for a while. So I was taking my suboxone to prolong the lingering sickness. I only had one prescription though, and needed to find a new doctor nearby.

With my new South Dakota-friendly phone and cell service, I quickly found out that there are 0 suboxone doctors in the state of South Dakota.

Zero. Nada. None.

I probably should've planned this better, but every part of my story seems to happen for a reason. I realized that opiates are not a problem in this particular region of the country. I'm sure you can find it, there somewhere, but it was not nearly as common in big sky country as it was in the big cities. There was just an absence of need for suboxone doctors or clinics.

This presented a problem.

I had come with only enough suboxone for 30 days, which I could stretch out a little bit and try to wean off of.

As Dan was thriving at his new job, reuniting with his brother, and loving mountain life; I was deeply struggling as I did not get along with Michelle. I think we both tried in our own ways. It was probably as uncomfortable for her as it was for me. And everyone fights their own battle which we know nothing about. I didn't know then that she was struggling too.

It didn't take long for us to realize we needed our own space. We found a cheap bottom half of a duplex just a couple streets away from Brian & Michelle, so Dan could still ride with him to work and we could have their help getting to grocery stores and such with no vehicle. Everyone we knew, we met through them.

It was a small town, you've probably heard of it.

Good old, Deadwood, South Dakota. Home of Wild Bill & Calamity Jane. Just a few minutes from Sturgis' famous motorcycle Rally.

Probably a lovely place to visit or vacation. There are many popular casinos all throughout the town, and little boutiques, and shops. They have weekly reenactments of the infamous Wild Bill shooting and a mock trial. We lived just one hour from Mount Rushmore. And from a distance the mountains were beautiful.

Most people that lived there loved it. But mountain life was just not for me. The weather is bi-polar, -5 in the morning and 75 in the afternoon, on any given day. The only common sense in this town was the name of the gas station. We didn't have a car for the majority of the time we lived there, and I was back to being 30 minutes from the nearest Walmart.

At one point, my mom sent us bicycles as a gift for something. It was so sweet and they were delivered brand new in boxes. The only problem was that you absolutely cannot ride a bike where we lived. I mean, you could try, but for one thing, you definitely need a helmet because you flew fast downhill on what could be ice or snow at any time, and for another, you couldn't get back uphill. Unless you were OK with walking your bike back home.

Chapter 24

Backwards

B y this time, I was out of my suboxone and had no chance of getting any more.

I was getting sick and frustrated. Secluded and stranded.

Someone I knew from back home had a Vicodin prescription she wasn't using and offered it to me.

I thought: "Okay, I can work with this."

But I knew that if I had 30 pills sent to me all at once, I'd do all of them. And then I'd be right back where I started.

This next method was admittedly a little crazy, and I don't necessarily recommend it, but it did work. I had my friend send me three a day for the first week, in the mail. Then two a day for the following week, in 7 days.

Once a week, I anxiously awaited the snow-covered mailman to bring my envelope of salvation. I saw the pills and immediately gobbled down two. Then had to really get a grip on the situation because I could not screw this up. They weren't coming any sooner than scheduled. And this was it.

I did this for 4 weeks.

Waiting for an envelope to bring me fewer and fewer pills. I was doing great limiting myself, sometimes I would run out a day or two early, but I'd learn my lesson and have to just sit and feel crummy until the next package arrived.

Soon, I took ½ a pill a day for 7 days, and no more.

And that was it.

I had used an opiate to get off of an opiate suppressor that was prescribed to get me off of an opiate (maybe that should've been the title of my book?).

I had successfully kicked it.

Finally, I didn't need something every day to survive. I wasn't sick. I felt human. This was an improvement, but I was still feeling extremely lost and lonely.

For a little while, I did ok without anything constant. I even got a job as a karaoke jockey at one of the popular bars in town. That was amazing, all that singing in my life had paid off. What a thrill it was to be on a stage, with my clothes on, doing something I absolutely loved.

That will forever be my favorite part of South Dakota.

It took a lot of guts to sing in front of large groups of people, especially without my opiate mask. Dan would come to watch me a lot of nights and we would sing together, drink, buy cigarettes out of vending machines, and have so much fun. And at the end of the night we would take a cab uphill back home.

Chapter 25

Meth

M ost of the people we knew, if not all, were using Meth. Every part of the map has an affliction unique to it's area and this was the rust belt's heroin equivalent.

If you're incognizant of drugs of this caliber; there are basically uppers and downers. Heroin, and other opiates, are downers. They "chill" you out, and calm you down.

Uppers, like cocaine and meth, race in the opposite direction and wire you up. Give you "energy" and loads of artificial pep. And while I had smoked crack and snorted cocaine in the past, during the strip club days, I had never tried meth. For me personally, I never liked uppers. I feel wired in my head all the time, and constantly have thoughts rushing and racing, so they didn't have as much appeal to me.

Not that that would stop me.

It didn't take long to be offered a pipe one night. It was a difficult task to tweek that was a two person job. Someone had to constantly keep the long white pipe heated while the other hit it.

I knew absolutely nothing about this substance or how to use it but, "ok, let's go".

It was fun at first.

It made everyone seem to like everyone more.

Suddenly it felt like I had friends in the area. We started off pretty slow because we didn't really go out of our way to find it. It usually found us with everyone we knew. We would walk over to a friend's house and stay awake all night smoking, talking, and going under their house to walk through old gold mine shafts. We could easily stay awake for 3 days at a time.

Which grew to be confusing.

I remember one time when I was standing outside of Brian and Michelle's house, trying to get to Dan who was inside and they wouldn't let me in. I had my pillow for some reason and called my mom. I rambled to her all this crazy nonsense and I remember arguing that it was 7 AM.

Although there is a time change, it's a 1-hour difference, not 13. She tried to explain to me that it was 7 PM.

Can you imagine this scenario?

I look back on that day and it's hard to believe I got the two of those confused.

I had lost 12 hours of a day and didn't even know it.

It was a strange drug. I didn't love it. I really didn't even like it honestly, but it turned me into something I wasn't. It gave me a mask to hide under. It gave me something more.

Dan and his brother both started working for another job, painting mostly. There was always a war between Michelle and me. We shared friends, since everyone we knew there, we met through them. And Dan and Brian worked together every day. It really wedged a deep chasm between us. Sometimes Dan would go visit them at their house just a few streets away, and I wouldn't be allowed to come. (Sound familiar?)

Chapter 26

Back To Jail (#4)

As the meth got me thinking about my old ways and addiction, and wasn't exactly wheting my whistle for more; I convinced someone from home to mail me a little bit of heroin.

I knew I couldn't get any more, so it was just a little treat.

It actually worked and I received a little packet in the mail.

I couldn't wait to do it.

Sadly, I didn't have a needle and decided that I would just go the route of snorting it. I was sure it would be good enough.

I don't know what followed.

Somehow, I ended up outside and completely naked.

Dan and I were fighting. I think it was about heroin. We were just outside our house when I saw police cars drive toward us. It was in the middle of the night, and again, for some reason I was naked. I ran back to our house and locked the door. Within minutes, officers were banging on the door, yelling my name. I ran into the other room, opened my packet, and shoved my nose into all the remaining heroin. And probably put clothes on. The police were not going away, and I eventually surrendered. I knew I'd be arrested because of my warrants. So as soon as they ran my name, I was off to jail.... Again.

I know that this theme is recurring...but this was the worst jail stay.

The first night and half of the next day I was basically passed out from the H I did before coming in.

I stayed in a medical pod because I was throwing up from doing so much. I think they just assumed that I was drunk and so I went with it.

This was the last time I ever used heroin. I had a feeling at the time it might be. I had hoped that it would be fun. One last hoorah. But this was not fun. I was back in jail. I didn't even get to enjoy it.

I was finally human enough to be let into the general population area. This was technically the county jail but it was so so small, that it was practically a city jail. There were only 5 cells with 2 beds each in our area. But before this stay, I always ended up in my own cell, being observed by the guards while I was withdrawing. At least I wasn't going to have to endure that whole ordeal again.

The cells were pretty full, and the girls were mean. Everyone knew everyone and I was the new girl. I was terrible at being in jail as my anxiety always went crazy. Even when I wasn't withdrawing this time, the minutes were like days. I wasn't going anywhere anytime soon, they told me they were waiting to hear from Ohio about my warrants. Someone told me it would probably take a couple of months to come to get me and take me to jail on my Ohio charges.

I needed a shower.

There were stalls across from our barred cells with shower curtains. Ok, so that's water.

But what about soap? Shampoo? Razor? Deodorant?

I hated asking anyone anything because they made me feel so stupid for not knowing. I discovered that you could buy all these things on your commissary but that takes time and money. I could get a start on that process but it would still be almost a week before I get my items.

You could order snacks, toothpaste, shampoo & conditioner, drink mix, instant coffee, coloring books, stamps, and calling cards.

I just wanted shower items and calling cards.

Razors could be checked out by a guard and used and returned, but only one day a week, which seemed to be the day before I asked for one.

They supplied you with a crappy toothbrush and toothpaste and deodorant that did absolutely nothing. I saw someone ask to use another girl's shampoo for her shower and I was terrified to ask but I did, and promised to reimburse a squirt when I got my commissary. She was less than kind about it but agreed. I have the thickest hair in the world and usually keep it long. So while shampoo & conditioner may seem silly to some, it was absolutely essential to me. Especially when you cannot use hair ties or rubber bands.

They would wake us up so early, maybe 5:30 in the morning, and we'd have to get up and get breakfast and sit outside of our cells. Wake up early and be miserable!! You weren't even allowed to just sleep the time away if you wanted to.

I read a book, I wish I knew what it was called because I never finished it and it's something I think of often.

I called my mom collect every chance I could (which is basically calling an operator that tells the person you are calling that they will be charged a lot of money for this phone call if they accept it. It's usually like $3 to accept and then plus an additional $1 per minute or something. It really adds up).

We had terrible meals, I would eat fruit and bread and give away my weird-colored slop mystery foods to the other girls.

If we were good, we could watch TV for one hour during the day, always controlled by this girl who was probably a little older than I was and definitely the leader of the group. She had been there for a few months and knew the system and routine better than anyone else there. She knew all the guards and they were nice to her. She was ferocious, to say the least. I'll never forget her. She only put on music videos and I remember her singing "Love never felt so good" The new song at the time that had been released by Justin Timberlake and Michael Jackson. This would forever be the theme song of Lawrence County Jail for me.

I was there for five whole days.

One morning, my name was called, and they told me Ohio changed the warrants to "in-state". And so I was going to be released.

You never realize how much you're hated by everyone else until they tell you that you're leaving.

Basically, I was too far away from Ohio, and would cost them more money and resources to come and get me than what my charges were worth.

Thank God.

I was released hours later, and Dan picked me up and took me home.

Chapter 27

Of My Dreams

A few months after I got out of jail, my mom and my brother came to visit us.

They saw our tiny duplex and met my puppy, Daisy, who was my Valentine's Day present from Dan. I got to show them the karaoke bar I worked at, and got to sing for them. We also went to Mount Rushmore for the first time!

It was a good visit but I was still very lost.

We were still doing meth at this time, I was drinking as much as I could tolerate, the feud was still going strong with Michelle, and my only piece of home was about to leave me. Thanks to my in-state warrants, I couldn't even go back with them if I wanted to. Plus, Dan was happy here.

A couple of years prior, we were staying in a hotel room in Detroit. And Dan, impulsively and romantically, poured his heart out to me and proposed.

I accepted in a heartbeat.

Since I had met him, I couldn't imagine my life without him. The next day, we went to a pawn shop and bought a ring. We never had a wedding date set, and never made big plans about one. Now we were in South Dakota away from both of our families, who I had always imagined would be at my wedding.

Back in South Dakota, my mom and my brother went back to the forbidden land of Ohio, and I stayed with Dan. I clung to him so tightly because he was my home. He was all I had. And I was terrified I'd lose him too. I just wanted to be married already. Something had to change and maybe this was it.

My family was more than supportive and we started our paperwork to make it official. We had a friend that was a minister and knew of a pretty park downtown in Deadwood where we could have a small ceremony.

As much as Dan wanted his family involved, there was just so much tension between Michelle and me that it made things difficult. So his family (also 30 hours away) didn't know what to think or who to believe in regards to myself or Michelle. And they were not as supportive. We had our Mine Shaft house friends be our witnesses. My puppy Daisy was our flower girl and on July 9th in Deadwood, South Dakota, Dan and I were married.

It was not the wedding of my dreams, I didn't have the dress of my dreams, and I didn't have the audience of my dreams.... This also wasn't the life of my dreams.

Being married changed absolutely nothing.

Dan and I fought and argued.

When Dan and Brian started working for this new job, I heard about their boss. He would give them meth to sell to earn some free for ourselves. All we had to do was sell half of it to one of our friends and it would pay for our share.

This went on for a while.

Sometimes Dan wouldn't get home until really late from work, because he was at Alex's house (his boss) and I'd patiently wait at home for his arrival so I could get high.

Michelle and Brian talked about Alex a lot too. It kind of seemed like everyone knew him except me. Even our mutual friends were always asking how he was doing.

Why hadn't I met him?

For a few months, he was a mystery man that seemed to really like Dan because he always just gave him a lot of cheap or complimentary meth to bring home.

The more drugs we had, the worse our relationship got. He was still working all day, and sometimes I'd walk downhill to visit a "friend" and oftentimes sold a little bit to him.

One of these friends was a guy who had a dog like my Daisy. I brought her over for a play date as we did our exchange. After a short conversation, I learned that he used to be into heroin as well, and he shoots up his meth.

That sounded crazy but he said it hits your system so hard that it's more like a downer than an upper.

What?

Had I been doing this wrong?

I got a few needles from him, tried it, and he was right. It was way different this way. We met up a few times to do this.

One day, I gave him what he was buying and he shot it up in maybe 2 minutes. I spent the following 2 hours in his bathroom because I couldn't find a vein. All of my veins had turned into scar tissue by this point from being derelict of use. He tried to help me find one and got just as annoyed at the process.

I gave up and mostly went back to smoking it. My withdrawal from this drug was so much more tolerable than opiates. I didn't get deathly ill, I didn't feel too bad. I just wanted more. And I cried a lot. I found this out one day when I decided to watch "My Girl". It wasn't the first time I'd seen the movie, and it probably wasn't even the fifth time I'd seen it, but my emotions flew into a wreck and I cried like a baby.

I finally was invited to Alex's house.

I'm not sure who exactly was keeping me away. But from what I had gathered, he was in a long-term relationship, was the main man of this company that Dan and Brian worked for, had affiliations with a huge motorcycle gang, and supplied us with meth.

The image that I had sketched together in my head was not at all what he was. He was a big guy, with a soft, kind face.

We entered his house from a side door to the basement. There were speakers everywhere! And couches and chairs in a circle and two microphones.

We took a seat and he offered us free reign over his stocked mini fridge. Intimidating bikers would stroll through occasionally to stay for a drink and do an exchange with Alex, and we'd go back to smoking and talking.

Sometimes there would be 3 pipes in rotation. By the time you exhaled, you were getting ready for another hit.

Then it happened.

Alex hooked his phone to this giant speaker system and turned on "Red Dirt Road" by Brooks & Dunn. He grabbed a microphone and passed one to his gangster friend that was always there- who was a little crazy, and about 100 years old.

They sang.

It was loud and wonderful.

I really couldn't think of anything better. It didn't take me very long to ask to sing. He would blast the music through the house, any song you wanted, and sing every chance he got. He would be mid-sentence, and stop to pull the microphone to his face to belt into it.

I loved this. I loved singing. I loved feeling accepted.

Chapter 28

Alex

I didn't think much of him at first. I loved the atmosphere, I loved partying with Dan all night. I loved singing. I loved the free drugs and I loved the power that went along with the association.

As Dan and I did more drugs and stayed up longer and longer, we fought more and more. Eventually, for some unknown reason, he stopped working for Alex.

One day, I thought I could write to Alex and ask if I could come to fence meth for the cost of product and then bring the money back shortly after.

I was shocked when he agreed.

I went by myself this time, picked up a batch from him, and sold half to earn half. I did this a couple of times before he told me I didn't have to pay him anymore.

Sometimes, I would take a cab to his place when Dan and I were fighting and he would pick up the fare and I'd jump into his singing circle.

I felt like I was right where I was supposed to be. And this is probably why everyone kept me away.

He noticed me one day (and his perception of these events probably differs greatly from mine) but I wasn't even trying to get his attention. I wasn't physically attracted to him. But everyone, and I mean *everyone*, was attracted to and gravitated toward his personality. He was hilarious, smart, connected, and had a seemingly endless supply of money.

Singing together frequently had a way of soothing my soul.

Sometimes I would get so wrapped up in the fun that I wouldn't return back home until early morning and as you can imagine, this created a lot of friction between Dan and me. These late nights that faded into dawn felt as if they were my slices of deserved time. Besides, he had enjoyed plenty of nights out while I sat at home alone, waiting for him.

Now that Dan no longer worked for Alex, he mentioned that he needed a painter.

I quickly asked if I could give it a shot. Again, he agreed and offered to pick me up the next morning.

I had to work alongside Dan's brother. Which stirred even greater the pot of chaos that was my marriage and the feud with Brian and Michelle.

Alex was protective, and he liked me for some reason. He thought I was going through a hard time and was helping me out by essentially letting me assume my husband's former position.

I was back to painting and loved it as much as before! And this time there was also the added bonus of unlimited meth! When I was with Alex, everyone was nicer to me. Accepting. He had this power over people. And he saw *me*. The more we talked and spent time together, the more we realized our similarities. Although he was far older than I was, he seemed to be the masculine version of myself. I have never felt aligned with someone the way I did with him.

I also never spent one day sober with him.

Dan was convinced something was going on between myself and Alex long before anything was. And I still can't figure out an appropriate word for our newly formed connection.

Lethal?

Dan and I attempted to separate.

Alex bought me a weekly hotel room, and this time it was fancy! He stayed at his house and I had this whole suite for just me and Daisy.

I now had unlimited time to spend trying to shoot up with a bottomless reservoir of meth. Blood stains began making their way onto the walls from unclogging clot-filled needles. Sheets began to collect rusty crimson puddles from where I'd pass out after doing a shot. Used needles piled up everywhere.

I stopped painting because Alex just gave me everything for free.

I'd go sing with him at his house and return back to my hotel room. Sometimes he would take me an hour away, to the big city. He would buy me dresses and makeup and outfits and I'd try them on and model them for him. He was my best friend. It was like hanging out with a mirror image of myself (a much wealthier mirror image). He took me out to high-class restaurants in my new clothes and jewelry. This was the life of my dreams.

Chapter 29

The Fence

I t really did feel like I won the lottery.

All the doors in South Dakota seemed to open for me with Alex's association.

I started riding with him to pick up his big batches. I was given phone numbers of important people he knew that I could always call in case I ever needed anything. All of our friends that we knew, now had to come to me to get their meth.

It felt intoxicatingly powerful. I felt adored. I was such a mess and this guy just gave me everything in exchange for nothing. The way he looked at me was like no one else ever has. Like he waited his whole life for me. We would finish each other's sentences. We would park his van and listen to music for hours. Silently falling in love with the songs. I think he was falling in love with me too.

Although this was the life of my dreams, Alex was not the man of my dreams.

My heart was still with Dan.

Who Alex was trying to help me get away from.

Dan was now home all day by himself while Alex painted, and I was just a few minutes down the road in a hotel room. I started asking

Dan to come over to hang out with me during the day. I tried to conceal it from Alex because I thought he'd stop giving me everything. The hotels, food, money, drugs, cigarettes, outings, casinos, and power would disappear.

When Dan came to my room, I loved sharing everything I had with him. Now we were in a fancy hotel room, we had unlimited meth, and I had new clothes and jewelry to look good for him.

But he would have to leave before Alex would show up.

It didn't take too long for Alex to find out that I was sneaking my husband into the hotel room that he was providing for me and sharing everything that he was giving me with the very same person I was supposed to be separating from.

This created yet even more issues with Dan because I loved him and I *did* want to be with him...but this new life was much more appealing.

Being with Alex was the first time I felt like South Dakota wouldn't be so bad.

It also caused tension with Alex because he was leaving his girlfriend of 20 years to pursue his feelings for me. But I didn't harvest the same feelings. I honestly tried to. It seemed as if life would've been easier with him.

If I could have just learned to love him.

"She's every woman" Garth Brooks

Do you know it? As you know already, I love music.

This was Alex's song to me:

"She's sun and rain, she's fire and ice

A little crazy but it's nice

And when she gets mad, you best leave her alone

'cause she'll rage just like a river

Then she'll beg you to forgive her

Ohhhhh! She's every woman that I've ever known

She's so New York and then L.A.

And every town along the way

She's every place that I've never been

She's makin' love on rainy nights

She's a stroll through Christmas lights

And she's everything I want to do again

And It needs no explanation

'Cause it all makes perfect sense

For when it comes down to temptation

She's on both sides of the fence

No, it needs no explanation

'Cause it all makes perfect sense

When it comes down to temptation

She's on both sides of the fence

She's anything but typical

She's so unpredictable

Oh but even at her worst it ain't that bad

She's as real as real can be

And she's every fantasy

Lord, she's every lover that I've ever had

And she's every lover that I've never had"

When it came down to temptation, I was on both sides of the fence.

For a couple of months, I secretly snuck away to be with Dan every chance I could.

While Alex kept searching for a connection that didn't exist.

Although I don't think I loved Alex, I loved myself being with Alex. I felt like who I had always wanted to be. The biggest problem was that I wanted to share that person whom I had always wanted to be...with Dan.

Chapter 30

Karma

D o you ever feel like something just slaps all of your plans in the face?

I was sitting at Alex's house singing one night, and out of nowhere, I was like, "Hmm. I haven't had my period in a while."

I had him take me to dollar general (where we were frequent shoppers) and bought some pregnancy tests. Back at Alex's house, I was sitting on the stairs to the basement, between the upstairs bathroom and the singing circle downstairs, waiting for the negative line to appear on the test. I couldn't tell you the date of my last period, couldn't even tell you the last time I ate, or at this point in my life, if it was even night or day.

Then not one, but two lines appear on this test in my hand. My first thought, my first impression, my first word ....Karma.

Of course, I would be pregnant.

Now.

Of all times.

I finally felt like I fit in. I finally had this guy giving me everything I could've dreamed of. I finally didn't need to chase money or drugs, they were being handed to me.

I was mad. Frustrated. Disappointed.

At first, I cried. I told Alex and he was supportive. He said everything would be okay. All I wanted to do was tell Dan. What was I
going to do? How could this be happening? I made my way back to
Dan as fast as I could. I told him the news and he was also conflicted
about the timing of it all. I was essentially living with another man,
and sneaking off to be with Dan and getting high with him at every
possible opportunity.

I left Dan to process this life-changing information and headed back
to Alex's house. I had a little bedroom set up there with Spider-Man
sheets along with my fancy outfits.

The fence I had been sitting on, now had an expiration date. And I
had to make a decision.

Shortly after I revealed the news to my Mom.

She was concerned and wanted me to come home.

She knew life at the time was a little crazy. Okay, it was very crazy for
me at the time. She knew I needed help and definitely couldn't have a
baby alone.

My heart chose Dan.

Dan knew it.

Alex knew it.

And I knew it all along.

Alex pleaded for me to stay with him, he offered me everything you
can imagine. He offered to support me and my baby.

He offered to buy me this red car I had been joyriding in occasionally.

His friend owned a car dealership and I was allowed to drive this
beautiful fast car whenever I wanted. I don't know how many times I
whipped around the mountain curves at 100 mph to get from Dan to
Alex and then back again.

In stark contrast, the car that Dan and I had, was a beater, and missing the handle for the driver's side door- so not only did we have to bungee around the thighs to keep the door closed, we couldn't even speed or make harsh turns because it would literally fly open.

So many things Alex offered me were appealing.

I really loved the life he was giving me. But if I hadn't found love *with* him at this point, I never would.

I loved Dan. Missed Dan. Wanted to have Dan's baby. Wanted to be with Dan.

Essentially I turned in my car keys and told Alex that I wanted to be with my husband, and cleared out my bedroom at his house.

Dan got a job on a guest ranch about 30 minutes from Alex's house back where we were living before.

It was in the middle of nowhere.

Dan worked during the day, getting the ranch ready for visitors and tourists so they could rent out a cabin or RV site. We were given a camper on the property to stay while he worked.

I was back to being secluded, lonely, and waiting for Dan to come home every day.

There was a convenience store across the street, I think it was a gas station too, but the only time I ever tried to get gas from there, the man said that they were waiting on a delivery. There was no gas. I had never heard of that before. At least never in Cleveland or Detroit. That little store was where we bought our food to cook every night over an open fire.

For a couple of weeks, we lived in this little camper. I cried a lot over the painful combination of withdrawing from the meth while gaining a ton of hormones in its absence.

We were supposed to be hidden, no one really knew where we went. But one day, Michelle showed up outside the camper, along with all of her dramatics.

I told her to leave. She yelled and called me fat. I'll never forget that, because, for the first time in my life, I was like "Yes! I'm fat, I'm pregnant stupid."

She told Alex where we were staying and he began popping up unexpectedly as well. And wouldn't you know it? He happened to know the owner of the guest ranch.

I hated being there.

I didn't feel like myself. I was bored. We had no money and Dan mostly worked on a barter system.

He was happy working at the ranch. Happy living on the ranch.

But I knew I needed more. My baby needed more.

I don't want this to sound easy, because it was the furthest thing from it. But I knew in my heart that I would not be able to stay sober in this state. I couldn't resist the constant temptation of running off to Alex for an easier life and free drugs. I would not be able to commit to my husband. I would not be able to provide a good life for my baby. I needed my mom. I needed to get away from Alex (not that he was so bad) but because I was so bad with him. Even if it felt so good. And what would happen if Alex got mad at me one day? And then I'm left with nothing? My baby and I would be out. Out on the street and my respect by association would vanish.

I had to go home.

I didn't know how to make that happen. I couldn't even go to Ohio without the fear of being arrested on my warrants. I couldn't go to jail.

Especially now.

Chapter 31

The Climb

I took another couple of weeks to convince Dan to leave with me. We were going to go back to Michigan, where his parents lived.

He wholeheartedly did not want to leave South Dakota as his perception of our time spent there differed greatly from mine. He loved it, while I despised it.

The day arrived. Finally, I would be leaving this awful state.

The beater was packed to its capacity and we switched the door handles so that we could actually close the driver's side door, which required us to permanently bolt one of the back seat doors shut because we needed the part. Daisy had a little spot in the back on top of everything we owned and we started our adventure towards home.

I'm not sure why a lot of things happened the way they did, and this was one of them. It felt like I was making the right choice, the best decision for myself and my future child, but after only an hour into the journey, our crappy car broke down.

I don't even remember what was wrong with it. I pulled into a shopping plaza and called the nearest repair shop. The man who answered the phone said: "Hey is this Alex? What's up, brother?"

I had been using one of Alex's old phones. Apparently, this guy was one of his many connections and he recognized the phone number. So that wasn't going to work. How was I still connected to him? We were trying to get away and still, South Dakota refused to let go...

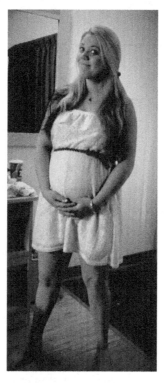

We switched to plan B and called Mom.

She and my brother were going to hop in the car and come to rescue us. But it was going to take 2 days to get to where we were. Fortunately, we had enough money for a hotel room to last us while we waited.

We cleared out the car and sold it for scrap and there were no unexpected interruptions at the hotel room. No people knocking on the door, police looking for us, gang friends keeping an eye out to see what I'm doing, or Michelle drama. Just me, Dan, and Daisy, and my tiny baby bump. I mean, fat. I saw the potential of a normal life together blossoming before me.

When my mom and brother arrived, we packed up their car but ended up having to ditch a lot of our things.

Bye-bye, Spider-Man bed set.

We just couldn't fit a carload of our items along with our dog plus 2 other canines along with four people. Their hasty departure left them with no time to make accommodations at a kennel. So we packed nothing but the essentials and headed for Michigan.

When we crossed the state line, under the big sign that said: "Leaving South Dakota", I felt this huge weight lift from my shoulders. A wave of relief washed over me. I promised myself I'd never go back.

We didn't have a plan, not even a blueprint. My only goal was to get away. I felt stuck in South Dakota. Trapped. And I knew at that time that I had to leave or I would never get out.

Upon arriving in Michigan, we went to another hotel room. It made me stop to realize that I had stayed in a lot of those in my life!

Dan's parents were confused, to say the least.

Brian and Michelle were feeding them all sorts of crazy stories. Mostly they came from Michelle, who was always trying to instigate dramatics and create a divide between us. They had known her longer than they had me. And my track record with Dan's family wasn't great so far. Michelle lived 30 hours from them so they only heard one side of the story from what she told them on the phone. His parents knew we were expecting, but also that we had just escaped from a literally crazy town, and had no plan. So we weren't welcome at their house just yet. Well, actually, it was just myself that wasn't welcomed.

Me (with my growing belly) and Daisy stayed sober in a hotel room just a few minutes from Dan's parent's house. Dan started working for a friend he knew from AA from the past. He was starting to make some money and we were looking into apartments or a place to rent nearby. We took the first affordable place that provided the greatest amount of convenience to his current job and accepted the house with such haste that we didn't even notice there wasn't a shower.

Life slowed down for us.

We were so humbled by our life at this time. We had a nice huge house that we were renting. We shared a car that Dan mostly used during the day to get to work. Whenever I needed something I would walk to the nearest gas station (back on flat land). I cooked dinner every night and had it waiting for when my husband would get home. I walked my dog. I finally saw a doctor, and my growing bump was doing great. We didn't have cable, we didn't have internet, and all of our furniture was from thrift stores or donated by the AA friend Dan was working for. We had this long flat coffee table in our living room, about 6 feet long and 1 foot high, that held our very small 19-inch tv where we could watch local channels with an antenna. Despite the lack of abundant luxuries we were sober and were happier than ever. We slowly started being accepted by my in-laws, as they saw our genuine attempt at a better life.

Then I broke that promise to myself.

Chapter 32

I Went Back

Dan and I had just picked up food (I think it was pizza?) and were sitting in the car when he got a call from Brian in South Dakota.

Michelle had been amidst a deep struggle with alcoholism, and tried to quit drinking on her own.... She sat in the same house that I had once lived in, and unfortunately, her organs failed before anyone realized the severity. She was rushed to the hospital where she died.

Dan spent hours on the phone with his brother, who was obviously heartbroken.

He planned to drive to South Dakota the following day with his mom.

I wasn't thrilled about him going but was actually more worried about being away from him while I was approaching 7 months pregnant. I was worried he wouldn't come back home without me. I begged to go along with them. So I went back to South Dakota. One last time.

We were only there for a few days. We stayed in a hotel room with Dan's Mom on the way there and Dan's Dad flew in to meet us. Once together, we stayed in a room with them while we were there. We mostly provided support for Brian during this difficult time. I made a poster board full of pictures of Michelle, to commemorate her life. This was also a humbling experience because she absolutely hated me. She hated that I got out, got away, and had bigger plans. I felt guilty that I was here and she wasn't. Guilty that we fought so much because she was battling a personal struggle as much as I was.

I was kind of keeping an eye out for Alex as we were back in this small town, I figured it would be impossible not to run into him. Some mutual acquaintances said that he had been in prison. Which was a relief. And also validated my choice in following my heart. What if I had chosen to stay with him? What would that mean for me and this huge belly of mine? What if we were living with him and counting on him and he went to prison?

I couldn't wait to get back home to Michigan, To my comfortable, safe, little home that had we made together.

3 months later, I went in to have my baby.

They freaked out about my blood pressure and ordered a cesarean section (C-section). My first thought was: "I'm going to die!" I had finally made it sober, was doing the right thing for my life and my child, and I wouldn't even be able to meet her.

But, in essence, I felt like I deserved it. I deserved way worse than a car breaking down on my way out of South Dakota, and perhaps a bounty of this magnitude was justly due.

My mom drove a swift 6 hours to see me before I went back for surgery. I cried so hard to her and was possibly the most scared I have ever been in my entire life. I had my mom promise me to take care of my baby, and always let her know that I loved her. I was certain I wouldn't make it. I somewhat felt like I didn't deserve to.

Chapter 33

My Baby

On a late November night, my daughter was born.

Dan and I were parents!! She was 8 pounds and 6 ounces of perfection. And mom was doing just fine! I held that tiny little girl, looking up at me with big blue eyes- looking into my heart, and changed me in an instant. I had made it. We made it. We were a family. We walked away from Hell on Earth, several times, conquered all the trials and tribulations of addiction, and were gifted this moment in exchange.

The definition of Karma: "Destiny or fate, following as effect from cause."

Do good, and you'll receive good back. Do bad, it's all bad. I was living proof of this. *She* was living proof. And so I named that sweet baby girl, Karma.

My little girl saved my life. And there's not a doubt in my mind about that fact. At that moment, holding that little human I created, I realized that everything in my life; all of the bad, all of my struggles, and heartache, led me to her.

Not that I am advocating pregnancy if you are in the throes of addiction. And I don't think that in my situation it was just an easy fix. I was ready and she gave me the motivation I needed to finally do something about it. You have to be ready to quit chasing the monster, and you'll never know if you are until you try to quit. And then try again. And again. And again. And again. It might not happen on your first attempt or even your tenth, but you owe it to yourself to keep trying. Every single day, just know that there is more. Your Karma can be good or bad. That part is entirely up to YOU.

That baby in my belly was a promise of more. A promise of a better life. A promise of responsibility and maturity. That baby was a ticket out of South Dakota. The miraculous conduit that held my marriage together while we healed, which also took time.

In hindsight, it's rather easy to admit that with the way we were living at the time, staying sober during my pregnancy would've been impossible for me in South Dakota. I knew that, I didn't want it to be true, and for the first time in my life, I did something to help someone else that would hurt me and be so hard for me. I chose the hard road in the hope of a better life. I was so very tired from 10 years of active addiction. 10 years that I should've spent being a kid!! Being a young adult, going to college, earning a degree. I was behind everyone I went to school with because I literally lost 10 years and can barely recollect anything other than fragments.

That was the hardest part for me, leaving the place I felt like I had everything I wanted. The place where I could be high all day every day (was there even a difference in days?). The place where I didn't hold a job, didn't need to, where I was just given drugs all the time.

I had made a decision that I knew I *had* to make, and even though I didn't *want* to follow through, I did and made it for my karma.

You just have to find your karma.

If you are anything like me, you'll never get sober just for you. You have to reach for more until you can finally grab it.

A better more.

And maybe your more is rehab? Maybe it's through the church? Crafts and artistic expression? Maybe you want to volunteer with animals? Or submerge yourself in A.A. meetings? Maybe you need to lock yourself in a hotel room that can be rented by the week and withdraw via Pepto, Imodium, Ginger Ale, and the help of someone you can trust- (thanks Mom). Maybe it is necessary to move across the country, and literally start over, cutting ties with everyone you know. Maybe you try 100 different things until you find the one that sticks. Drastic measures produce lasting treasures. Please just keep trying.

IF I CAN DO THIS, I PROMISE YOU ANYONE CAN.

Having a baby is LIFE CHANGING in so many ways. We were living a few minutes from Dan's parents and had upgraded to renting a home (with a shower!). My mom, stepdad, brother, uncle, cousin, and grandma often drove 5 hours to come to visit us and spend time with the baby.

Having a little person that needs you 24/7 really changes your perspective. Dan worked all day while I kept the house clean, went grocery shopping, and watched Sesame Street & cooking shows with Karma. (At least we alternated and I didn't just give her a little box on the screen haha).

When Dan got home, we'd eat dinner and I'd watch them play together, then I'd go to bed and let them stay up together until the baby went to sleep. She slept in a little bassinet next to our bed for the first few months, and then we co-slept. I would put my arms in a big circle around her and sleep with one eye open so if she ever moved a limb, I'd feel her. I was head over heels in love with this baby. She was everything to me. Every single second of the day, she needed me. And oh did I also need her.

The more time that went on, the easier it was to stay sober. I had a completely new life and a little girl that was counting on me. She deserved everything this world had to offer. Being her mom, being accountable, and being responsible for the first time ever, felt so good.

Dan and I were so happy.

And so in love.

Sharing our little family of 3 plus Daisy, with his parents and my family back in Ohio brought me all the joy I could ever wish for.

We started making weekend trips to visit my family in Ohio, being really careful because of the old warrants.

I rekindled relationships with a lot (maybe even most) of my family members who had assumed that they would never see me again. Now, they saw me as a devoted mother and a wife, instead of high and passed out on the couch or calling from jail.

Life back in Michigan was slow, which we didn't mind at first. We spent a lot of time with my in-laws since they were close by. We had weekly dinners there, and my mother-in-law was absolutely wonderful with the baby which gave me some free time to shower or do laundry or just go for a walk.

But I still missed home and I hated driving away from Ohio on those weekend trips.

I started going home to my mom's house during the week for a few days. Where during that time, I'd visit my sisters and my grandma, then drive back home to Dan. And on the weekend, I'd go back and visit my other family. It was always a celebration, and so fun showing off Karma as she got older. Boy is she a firecracker!

My heart was pulling me back home. Karma and my mom have this crazy strong bond, I guess I asked for that. One grandma had just passed, and the other one was getting older; I had missed so much time with everyone already. And now I was normal. And I have this little girl I want them to know! But again, Dan wasn't ready to make a move. He went to work full-time and made friends in Michigan. My only friends were his parents. Not that I needed friends really, but I felt like I had 100 family members back home that I was cramming into 2-day visits, and spending 2 weeks with his 2 parents. Eventually, I started really considering coming home to live with my mom.

Chapter 34

Accountability

I decided that Karma, Daisy, and I would go live with my mom, and we would spend weekends visiting Dan or having him come to visit us there in Ohio.

One thing had to happen before I could be comfortable anywhere in this state. I was so scared every time I drove through Ohio to visit family, or parked my car at my mom's house, living with the persistent fear that some police car would see my name if they ever ran my plates and then I'd be arrested again because of my old warrants.

I was free just a few hours away in Michigan.

But as soon as I crossed into Ohio I felt the anxiety steadily increase. What would happen to my 2-year-old if I was arrested and we were in the car together? How could I ever think about putting her through that?!

I explained my situation to a couple of family members that contributed to an attorney fund for me and I was able to talk to this guy about my old charges and warrants and he would work with the system to get me in front of a judge and get everything wrapped up as fast as possible. I was chock full of optimism, because this time, I was sober, and doing the right thing. I was going to turn myself in, and they would all be proud of me.

Yeah, nope. Doesn't work like that.

I had a date set to turn myself in with my attorney. My mom took off work to be with my daughter, who I explained to that I had to go work for a few days.

Absolutely heartbreaking.

I had never been away from her for longer than just overnight. But I knew I had to do this. I knew it would be okay.

The attorney said I would probably be in jail for 3 days. "Ok, 3 days. I can do this." Three days in jail without the burden of enduring withdrawal symptoms? Piece of cake!

I woke up at 6 AM and showered and skipped the coffee, as there was no point in spiking energy for that day. I was dropped off at the local police department to meet my attorney at 7 AM. I had only talked to him on the phone until now since I lived out of state. There were several warrants in different districts and he had a plan as to where we would start the process.

I believe the first charge I turned myself in for was petty theft. About 5 years prior to this point in time, I had been working a hustle pretty regularly at a popular store. I would take clothing items off the rack, run them upstairs as if I were returning them for store credit, then off the profits for 50% of the value in cash.

One of the times they caught me.

I spent the first few hours in that small jail right by my mom's house. Mostly napped because I didn't have coffee, and it was early. I saw a virtual judge and was given fines and fees. Then I was moved to the county jail downtown. The officers who transported me were so nice and treated me like a human. Everything was moving quickly so far, and it looked promising. Until...

Chapter 35

Cuyahoga County Jail (#5)

We entered the jail through a large basement garage. The garage door closed behind the police car as it pulled in. I saw the guards come out of the building and put their weapons in a locked box on the wall. They exchanged paperwork with the officers that escorted me and then opened my car door. I was taken inside the jail, which was absolutely huge. I had only been to small jails up until then. This was the big Downtown Cleveland, County jail. 26 stories high.

There were 2 things that were getting me through this:

1- I wouldn't be in withdrawal, so it couldn't be as bad as before

2- I was turning myself in. And they were going to care.

What foolish hunches those turned out to be.

I was given an outfit to put on and a white t-shirt and knock-off crocs that were 4 sizes too big for my feet which forced me into waddling.

They said they were all they had.

They were not kind, they were quite the opposite. During a very long and tedious check-in process, this woman asked me how long I'm staying (do I get to choose?).

"Not long, just a few days."

"Not with these charges" she giggled.

Suddenly I wasn't so confident, but she didn't know my attorney.

"Yeah, but I turned myself in!!" I replied proudly.

She only laughed harder.

I finally made it to one of those very high stories. I have no idea what floor it was (they probably try to keep you from knowing too much information in there). We could see the tops of several buildings. I shuffled in my huge clogs as I was being rushed by this mean lady. She handed over my folder to another lady who looked like she was having a bad day. The new mean lady guard takes me to a room to get a "mattress" (think middle school gym mat). I grabbed one and then she gave me a crusty blanket and towel, a toothbrush, and a bar of soap

She then rattled off this little saying that I feel like she says to everyone that comes in. Not that this is verbatim, but it went something like: "No f**king, no fighting, no eating coochie, keep your hands to yourself cuz I ain't no captain save-a-hoe". Such helpful advice....

We entered a giant cell that had 2 metal bunk beds back to back on the left wall, a small space with windows on the back wall, and another 2 bunk beds back to back on the right wall.

"They're out of beds...so you'll have to take the floor." She told me with indifference.

Perfect.

I put my gym mat mattress on the floor on the opposite wall of the windows, right next to the cell door. The door was open during most of the day, to get to the bathroom. You could shower but only at designated times and could watch tv for an hour in the evening if everyone on the floor behaved- which was completely out of my control. I just tried to keep my head down to get through this and back home to my baby girl with no scars.

But I was the new girl on the floor in this giant cell with 8 other women. And as much as I wanted to keep to myself, they kept asking me questions.

The girls in my cell were there for various reasons; some were waiting on court dates, some were sitting out their sentences, and most had been in there for a few months at least. The more I told them of my situation, the more they hated me. They didn't have money for attorneys and they definitely didn't turn themselves in, they were caught. I was pretty confident that I'd get out in 3 days but was trying to keep it to myself. I had mentioned my past heroin use and that I was sober now. I made a big deal out of that, because it was a big deal, and this was going to be so easy this time!

I couldn't sleep the first night. I have back problems and sleeping on the cement floor wasn't helping. I had terrible anxiety. I wanted to smoke a cigarette. I wanted my daughter.

I went to use the restroom and there was a line outside the door in front of the guard desk. The guard woman had told me that there was a 3-person limit at a time. I saw 2 pairs of feet in the stalls and I went into another. I sat down on the toilet to go. The metal was absolutely freezing and uncomfortable.

The guard came in screaming: "There is a 2-person limit! Get out now!"

I hurriedly got dressed and surmised that I'd be skipping the bathroom that morning.

I was frazzled and apologized and tried explaining that I was told it was a 3-person limit and that's why I went in.

My explanations fell on deaf ears.

She scolded me, made me feel stupid, degraded me, and said: "Maybe that's how it is with the other guard. Now I'm on duty, and this is MY rule!"

What!?

Was I supposed to remember each guard and their own rules?!

I started sneezing. Like a lot. Which is a common first sign of withdrawal. I made a whole thing about not being on anything anymore but suddenly my physical appearance was saying otherwise. By the 2nd day I was sweating terribly- rubbing a bar of soap on my armpits since that's all I had to work with. I was shaking and sneezing. I was clearly withdrawing.

I didn't plan on calling home at all during this time, since we knew it would be just 3 short days. But something was wrong. I called my mom the 2nd day around noon when our cell doors opened and we were allowed to use the main area. I told her I was withdrawing. I was sick and I didn't know why. We sat there on the phone trying to think of what was going on- she knew I wasn't using! I thought it was cigarettes at first.

Then it hit me.

For the past couple of years I had been taking Ativan for anxiety and to help me sleep. One each night at bedtime. I never felt like it affected me otherwise. I didn't even consider it, it was prescribed. But in that jail cell, I realized that my body was very much addicted to this substance. There wasn't anything I could do about it at that point.

I was mad.

Disappointed.

Angry.

And I looked like a liar.

This was supposed to be different this time. Easier. It felt like I was being punished for doing the right thing. I couldn't understand why it happened this way to me. I was trying to be accountable and make amends and start fresh for my daughter. Why then the additional challenge?!

I'm grateful now that everything happened the way it did. I truly honestly didn't know I was addicted or reliant on anything when I went into jail. Obviously, I wouldn't have made myself withdraw there on purpose. Those pills were taking a part of me each night when I took them; and yes, they helped with my anxiety; and yes, they were prescribed by a doctor- but...I am an addict. And I don't ever want to be physically dependent on ANYTHING ever again. So I promised myself I wouldn't ever take it again, and I didn't.

Back in jail, after having told my cell mates that I was this reformed golden child who had turned herself in on old heroin charges that was so much better, and now a sober mother... I was deep in withdrawal from a benzodiazepine.

I had only ever heard of this withdrawal since I was more familiar with opiates. And the withdrawals do differ per substance. It was similar in a lot of ways, but mostly I was trying to hide it and the disappointment in myself with the realization of my dependence. I believe this is the most dangerous category of drugs to withdraw from. And I didn't even mean to be taking it.

My attorney came to see me that same day, I was trying to act like I was as normal as the day before when he saw me. He said everything was moving pretty well on his end, that he was waiting on some things to happen and then we would go in front of another judge, and that I'd be out. Hopefully by the following day.

The days were very long.

I was treated like an outcast at every moment.

Whenever I said something or did something it was wrong. I walked too slowly in my oversized shoes and was scolded. I even got yelled at for having shoes that were far too big for me (as if it were my choice!) If I sat down, I picked the wrong chair. If I tried to nap, I was told we had to be awake.

It was extremely foolish of me to think anyone would care for one second that I turned myself in. It was foolish to think anyone would look at my file and see that the charges were from years ago.

Picture this: you're a 20-year-old homeless man and are starving. You get caught stealing a chicken sandwich from the gas station and are then taken to jail.

Now, picture this: a 20-year-old man just shot and killed his mother. Arrested and taken to jail.

Those two people are treated with indifference to the charges. No one opens your file. And they certainly don't check the dates or severity of your charges.

Not only was my freedom surrendered, but also any and all respect.

I didn't eat anything while I was there. I was so hungry but I couldn't fathom ingesting what they served us. I would put my plate in the middle of the cell floor and the other girls would flock to it like pigs to a trough. I probably lost 10 lbs during that stay.

On the third day, I was feeling hopeful.

Finally, I'd be getting home to my baby. The morning started early as usual, 5 AM, to look at the "breakfast" I wouldn't be eating and stare at the walls.

No sleeping or napping allowed.

By the afternoon, I was called down to go to court. I was in small a room with maybe 10 other people who were absolutely terrifying. Usually, men and women are separated. But for court, they lumped us all together to take turns on a video call with the judge.

Eventually, my name was called, it was short and sweet. I was also given fines and fees and a court date for my last outstanding warrant in a different district. I would be released that day.

I made my way back to my cell to be questioned by the other girls. I knew they wouldn't like what I had to say, but I told them I was pretty sure I'd be leaving.

Until that point, they had doubted the reality of my attorney's plan, so much so that I had begun to as well.

I sat there waiting for my name to be called.

Lunch was served, dinner was served, and I was still waiting.

I finally called my mom to ask what was going on! She told me that they were having all kinds of problems getting me released. As soon as the paperwork was being processed, someone flagged it because my attorney had changed from the original court-appointed attorney (from when I was arrested 5 years prior to this point) to this new guy that my family helped me hire. They weren't sure how fast they could fix this. (Oh sure, now they look at the dates).

I was released that night.

It was a long process, maybe 3 hours of moving from holding cell to holding cell on different floors.

Eventually, I was put in a cell with 6 or 7 other girls that were being released as well. We were given our clothes and belongings and finally, they took us to the front door to walk out.

I didn't bring any belongings since I planned on being transferred around and gone for a few days. I borrowed a phone from one of the girls in my release cell and called my mom who said my brother would be on his way to come get me. I actually planned on quitting smoking cigarettes while I was in because I knew after 3 days of not having one, it would be easy. But after the additional stress and unexpected challenge of withdrawing from a drug that I didn't know I was depending on- I ended up bumming one from someone while I waited for my ride home.

My brother picked me up and we went to Panda Express. I had 3 and a half days of eating to make up for. We took the food home to my mom's, where I hugged my baby girl so hard, and then took a long hot shower.

A couple of days later, I was expected to go to court for my last outstanding warrant. This was for the drug instruments and possession of heroin (remember when I woke up in the truck with police outside and was charged with heroin even though I didn't have any?).

This was 5-6 years ago at this point. I went to court, met my attorney, and waited to be called in front of the judge. This was it, finally, someone was going to be proud of me for turning myself in. I was one of the first people called since I had representation. My attorney did most of the talking while I added the obligatory "Yes your honor" and "No your honor".

The judge was not proud of me, and I don't think he looked at the file or dates or anything very well.

He probably only saw the charges and the deals I had just made with the county jail to pay fines and fees and had spent 3 days in and got this court date.

The only thing he said to me was: "I hope you can address your demons".

I stood mute.

In my head, I was yelling "THAT'S WHAT I AM DOING RIGHT NOW!!"

I walked away from the podium with my attorney that was satisfied with our 5-minute appearance with the judge. In my head, I was just repeating "Address your demons". I needed validation and thought I was going to get it from someone. That's when I realized I was proud of myself, and that that was enough.

I went outside to the police department parking lot and took a selfie with one of the police cars. Why? Because I could. Because I was allowed to be in that parking lot, because I was allowed to be in that city, in that state. Because I could give my name to anyone in the world and not be hauled away in handcuffs. Because I DID address my demons.

That selfie was my validation.

I had this thousand-pound weight lifted off my shoulders as I drove back home to my daughter. We could finally go to the zoo, the movies, visit family, and go grocery shopping, without my fear of being taken away from her and putting her through an undeniably stressful situation. Plus, if I had been caught on my warrants, I would've been sentenced to far longer. It probably would've been closer to a year than 3 days.

Chapter 36

Freedom

I was finally free.

I felt so proud of myself. I had weaned myself off of the Ativan that I had unknowingly become addicted to and was confident and determined never to go back to the shelter of any kind of dope.

I felt good. Healthy. Happy.

I drove my daughter all over the once-forbidden state of Ohio, visiting everyone we knew.

Every day felt like a holiday!

I was so so happy to be home. We spent weekends visiting Dan in Michigan or he'd come and visit us at my mom's house.

One day, my (now) sister-in-law invited me and my mom to a free "makeup party", so we said yes. Why not?

That next Thursday evening, My mom, my sister-in-law, and I walked into this pretty little studio that was outfitted with comfy pink couches and had mirrors everywhere. Other women were arriving as well, and we took our seats at a table. We were asked a couple of questions about our skin and makeup routine and were given some products on a tray in front of us.

I never dreamed this evening would change my life, but it did.

We took off our makeup and used the products as we learned about how and when to use them and the positive beneficiaries to our skin.

It was fun and frilly and lighthearted and the complete opposite of jail.

My mom planned on buying some of the products after the skin-care party, so we stayed around to talk to the women in charge. The two women who hosted both drove free cars from the company they worked for, had amazing purses, beautifully done nails, and they were like...really pretty.

The women eventually made their way to our table, and the one who owned the studio suggested that instead of my mom buying products from them, I should sign up and she could then buy directly from me.

"Oh no, I can't, I have a 2-year-old,"

"I do too, they will be best friends!" She responded.

My mom and I sat there for a moment.

I didn't have any money, and it cost a bit to join. But my Mom took one look at the expression on my face, and at that moment, she knew that this was what I wanted to do.

She confidently handed over her credit card so I could begin this new endeavor. The studio owner invited me to come over to her house down the street on the following day for her team's weekly meeting and even added that I should bring my baby!

Chapter 37

Do It Anyway

I was nervous when I went to that first meeting.

But my baby was watching me, so I held my head high and did it anyway.

Karma and I parked on the street and walked up to the address provided. The house was huge! Probably the most beautiful home I had ever been in. I was greeted at the door by the woman who owned the studio. She embraced me with a hug and then kneeled on the floor to talk to my daughter.

Next, she walked us into the other room where there were 20 other women with notebooks, laptops, cellphones, and a spread of yummy food.

Karma met the woman's daughter. It turned out that she was the same age and so they went to play in the playroom.

I was introduced to the other women, and have never in my life felt so accepted. They were so nice! Motivated and determined and happy and lighthearted and fun. It felt contagious. And so in true Rachel fashion, even though I really had no idea what I was doing, I just kind of jumped in.

I officially had my own business.

I was taught the basics of how to reach out to people both online and in the neighborhood to offer them free pampering services at the studio. Much like the same as I had gone to.

My first party was mostly a couple of my mom's friends who came out to support me. I think I sold nearly $400 of products in 2 hours, which made me a profit of $100/hour.

Ok, we might be onto something here.

I reinvested all of my profit from the first few parties into inventory.

Some people (friends, and family) thought this was crazy. And admittedly, I oftentimes did too. I mean, who was I to think that I could do any of this?!

But every time I'd walk into that studio, or my mentor's house for weekly meetings, my faith was restored. So I did it anyway.

Their genuine belief in my potential helped to inspire me to continue going forward with confidence.

When I held those free pampering parties, I'd get to the studio before the appointment time, unlock the door, and get set up.

I was always ready to sell with my hair and makeup done, my beauty coat on, and my dress (thanks Goodwill) and dress shoes on to complete the ensemble.

Women would come to meet me at their designated appointment time and bring two friends along.

They were a wide variety of life.

Doctors, nurses, lawyers, teachers, moms, grandmas, teenagers, construction workers, etc... who I got to teach about skincare.

I enjoyed every second of every party I held.

And I still do.

I never dreamed I'd have my own business. I never dreamed I'd be passionate about washing one's face. But it really is so much more than just that. Finally, a *good* more. I was providing a service, I was teaching women about their skin and the most suitable products to use. I was selling makeup—and everything you can imagine was in the back of my car and ready to sell for any eyeliner emergencies.

I began to find value in myself.

I found a reason to get out of the house and be more than just a Mom for 2 hours (Not that being a mom isn't the absolute best thing in the world, but sometimes you need to have an adult conversation!). I found friends- True, true, lifelong, friends. I found income and independence! I really found myself.

I started holding regular evening appointments at the studio when my mom could watch Karma.

Dan was ready to make the move to Ohio because I think he realized that I was thriving in my newfound position and had no plans of returning to Michigan.

He moved into my mom's house with us and started a new job. I would wait for him to get home, and then rush off to work my business.

I was generating a profit at 90% of those appointments. And even when I didn't make money, I still felt as if I were valued and a contributing member of society.

Sometimes it even just felt like I was hanging out with friends!

Once finished, I would return home to my little family, who missed me in that short time away.

I was constantly winning prizes and awards and jewelry and recognition from my new team. Rewards for actually being pretty good at this! I was never bored anymore, because I had a thousand things I could be doing to grow my business (In between being a full-time mom, of course).

A few months later, after we established a routine with my business and Dan's full-time job in our new area, we started renting our own home. A few minutes down the street from where my Mom lived.

Two years later, we decided that we wanted to grow our family and I became pregnant with a second child.

My son.

We decided to name him after my Dad. And he came out looking exactly like him, healing a piece of my heart.

Chapter 38

Today

L et me tell you about my life today: I am 32 years old, a home-maker, a small business owner, and a hardworking momma to two beautiful children, and two dogs (one has passed since I started writing this book; which was honestly one of the hardest things I've ever gone through).

The only hours I count are for sleep schedules. The only powder on my counter is translucent. I have several bank accounts, and my nails are always done (sparkly grey at the moment). I have a few hundred dollars of inventory for my business on any given day. I have close to 10 designer bags (LV, Ralph Lauren, Michael Kors, Coach, and Kate Spade). I have a car. I have been placed in the top 10 consultants for sales in my unit every year since I joined. I have jewelry (a lot of it!). I have friends. Really good friends! I am sending myself to another country for a girl's trip next month with cash I have been saving in a box for 6 months. I am able to sign my daughter up for Girl Scouts, soccer, softball, theater, gymnastics, summer camp, and safety town; and I will be her cheerleader in all she does.

And, most importantly, I now have my family back.

I spend my days cleaning, packing lunches, cooking (I love to cook!), gardening, swimming in the pool, going to beaches, or just being silly with my kids. I am fortunate to be able to stay at home with them and watch them grow. I cram as much of my cosmetics business into my spare time as possible. We go out of state on family vacations and have just gotten a new car!

I'm not telling you these things to brag. And maybe to you the reader, it may not seem like much. But none of this was possible for me 10 years ago.

During the eye of the storm, I never had a dollar to my name. Anything with remote value would end up at a pawn shop. I had no bank account and couldn't leave the state or stray too far from the tether of my dealer because before long I would always need a fix.

I had zero friends. And I hated myself.

I look at my kids and I am so grateful to myself for making that change.

I admire their little hands and squishy faces. I am so blessed to have what I have. I am humbled by their love for me every day and I can't believe I almost missed this.

I am so lucky.

Even on the days when I feel like life is against me. When I am up all night with the kids and have a stomach ache of my own, or I spill my coffee on the floor and I even sit down and have a good cry about it. I am *still* so grateful to be alive to experience all of these moments.

I am confident in my strength now. I know I can handle anything that comes my way because, with the durability attained from a battle that almost cost me everything, I feel that I have already survived hell. I know I am strong enough to push forward and to just keep swimming. Even on those hard days.

I could let it go. I could sit here silently sober for the rest of my life, and nobody would ever have to know.

But that isn't helping anyone.

If everyone that achieved the miracle of sobriety had stayed quiet about their journey, there would be no awareness or programs to help those in active addiction.

I can't sit quietly.

I won't watch my friends die knowing I could've possibly changed just one of their minds with my story.

Chapter 39

Choose your hard

People say being a mom is the hardest job there is.

It's not.

Being an addict is.

Chasing something that will never love you or give you anything, is extremely hard. Having to constantly lie and manipulate your way through life, that is hard. Spending hours in a bathroom, fighting scar tissue and blood clots to eventually waste your only $10 shot of heroin, is hard. When most of your family accepts that they have lost you and will likely never see you again—that is hard. Being so sick every 8 hours of your life to where you will lie, cheat, and steal your way to health—that is hard. Hiding yourself and your track marks— that is hard. Losing days, weeks, months, and years to addiction—that is hard. Dodging warrants and going to jail—that is hard. Not having a home—that is hard. Not having any friends—that is hard. Not having any self-worth or value in yourself—that is hard. In summation, the journey with addiction was the hardest thing I ever had to go through.

And I'm not going back.

Staying sober is easy for me now. It really really is. I've worked hard to create a life without temptation. I am never in a situation where I'd be around drugs or that darkness. And if I was, I am 100% confident in removing myself from it. I have come too far to let myself fall. My life isn't about me anymore, it's about my children. I lost a parent when I was so young, and I will stay on this planet as long as I can for them.

Although this is my story, I feel that it is important to share that my husband has struggled with sobriety a few times since my daughter was born.

I have seen firsthand how easily we can fall back into old habits and I cannot change anyone that doesn't want to be changed.

I hope you do.

I pray that all addicts can see how beautiful each day can be when you aren't living in turmoil. I have seen how very important it is to share your experiences. To be honest and open about your addiction, and to be extremely cautious of who you let in your life.

I feel like that is what separates my experience from my husband's. I have kept to myself and focused on my family. I place a tremendous amount of value in examination and carefully select each and every person I let into my life. I have been honest about my past and have been accepted for it.

There is an overwhelming sense of liberation, a feeling of freedom in knowing that I will be sober tomorrow, I will be sober next week, and I will be sober next year.

I know that, 100%.

At the end of the day; I am my person.

This is my life.

If I used again, it would kill me. I know that for sure. And I have shown myself time and time again that one thing won't be enough and I'll always go back to searching for more.

So I just won't.

Not even when he does.

Not even when I'm alone.

Not even when I'm heartbroken.

Not even when I lose my 15-year-old dog who meant the world to me.

It. Has. Never. Crossed. My. Mind.

If you met me today, you'd never know anything of my past. I have had this all on my chest for nearly ten years and felt the need to share my story in hopes of inspiring other addicts to get clean.

So I wrote a book!

The day after I told Karma I was writing a book about my life, she brought home a stack of glued papers from school. The front page said, "Karma's buk" (Kindergarten speak). I sent a picture to my mom, and said "She wants to be just like me, so I have to be great!".

I owe so much to my mom, for sticking by me through everything. I could never say sorry enough for all the sleepless nights I gave her. For all the crazed phone calls that she never missed. For all of the times that I manipulated her and stole from her. Most of which I don't even remember. For always supporting me no matter where I was, and for believing I could be more.

Today, my mom is my absolute best friend.

We have the best relationship! She lives 7 minutes from me and we text constantly, there is never a day I don't talk to her. She is the only one who saw me at my worst time and time again, and somehow still loved me and saw potential in life for me after addiction. She believed in me when I didn't. She still is my biggest cheerleader when it comes to anything. Thank you, Mom.

For those who are struggling. You can literally do anything you put your mind to. You *can* get sober and you *can* stay sober. I understand, I have been where you are. I cannot imagine being shocked at anyone's story, because I've done it all. If there is one thing I can promise you, it is this: that I've been to the lowest of lows.

But that doesn't have to be your whole story, just a chapter.

Chapter 40

I Am Alive

Living in active addiction for a decade left me with long-term consequences that I am forced to deal with every day.

But I am alive.

Opiates weaken your bones, so I have had to have several surgeries to fix or replace my teeth. Which took time and money.

But I am alive.

I have sciatica, spinal degeneration, and arthritis of the spine—it hurts every second of every day. My lower back and leg are constantly radiating pain. One of my doctors said my X-rays show severe whiplash from about ten years ago. Who knows? It's anybody's guess, the way I was living my life.

But I am alive.

I have scars and scar tissue on my hands and wrists and arms that will always be there. Getting bloodwork done has become an embarrassing, difficult, and shameful process.

But I am alive.

I have an unappealing criminal record that will follow me forever.

But I am alive.

I have guilt, for the people I hurt and the things I've done. I've made amends and been forgiven by everyone (which also took time) except myself—which I think is partly a good thing. It's a constant reminder of how much better my life is today, and that I never want to be that person again.

But I am alive.

Chapter 41

To The Addict

I know you want to get out. I know you want more. I know you are tired.

I wrote my story because, even though many people will now know the worst things about me, you will too.

But today my life is truly wonderful!

And yours can be too!

I believe in you, without even knowing you. Because I am certain I am not special. I am certain I am not one of a kind. I am not strong—no stronger than you. You can make a new life. It is hard. It takes work and time. It takes faith in something bigger than yourself.

Find it.

Every day it comes down to a choice. Believe me, I know it's not an easy one, but it's still a choice. You have to CHOOSE to be better. Choose rehab—there are so many more options and resources available today than there were when I needed help. There are free inpatient rehabs. There are sober homes where they will help you get jobs and provide the supervision you need until you're strong enough to get off the fence.

I know it's hard to imagine, I know it might seem impossible. My story is in no way a how-to book. Your story won't be exactly like mine, or anyone else's. But the fact is, you're the author. You can write anything you want in your story.

If you are reading this, it's not too late. Make the choice to better yourself. Give yourself more. You deserve it, even if you don't think so. Your future self will thank you.

Do it for your Mom. Do it for your Dad.

Do it for the siblings you stole from.

Do it for your Grandma you lost time with.

Do it for your future babies.

Do it for that little girl or boy you used to be, that aspired for greatness.

Aspire again.

Do it for all of the people you know that didn't get a chance to.

Just do it!

Resources for help

I highly recommend startyourrecovery.org for resources on treatment centers in your area that accept insurance, no insurance, or Medicaid. Very well put together and helpful.

I've also started a Facebook group called "The Sober Clover" where I will continue to share quality resources, both for donating to the cause itself and for finding affordable and accessible treatment near you.

Resources to donate:

Safeproject.us
Donations: 100% tax deductible, non profit organization founded by the grieving parents of an overdose.
Articles on: what to do if you witness an overdose/ prevent an overdose, transitioning out of treatment. help for veterans, treatment & support locator.

rosecrance.org : non profit, fully licensed & accredited. Accepts many insurances and has a patient assistance program. Based in IL.

Isiah-house.org non profit, KY based, over 8 treatment centers, also o-
ffers college credits for patients. Nationally accredited & state licensed.

I found it incredibly difficult to find these websites and resources in
general so I'd like to make that easier for the public.